VAGUS NERVE VITALITY

THE ULTIMATE GUIDE TO IMPROVE GUT HEALTH, ALLEVIATE STRESS AND ACHIEVE OPTIMUM HEALTH IN JUST 10 MINUTES A DAY

NICOLE REAP

CONTENTS

INTRODUCTION

During a really tough time in my life when I was juggling menopause, dealing with a divorce, and trying to manage constant other stresses, I discovered something that truly turned things around for me: somatic therapy. It helped me heal and, even more importantly, completely shifted how I saw the connection between our bodies and minds.

Let me introduce myself. Hi, I'm Nicole Reap. Over the years, I've worn many hats—running my own businesses, teaching, and writing and publishing books. My journey has given me a deep appreciation for how understanding and caring for the connection between body and mind can be transformative. This book is a reflection of my experiences and insights, shared to help you boost your mental and physical well-being through easy yet powerful somatic exercises. It is also packed with science-based information and facts about healing our bodies with specific and simple exercises, techniques, and practices.

For example, "Vagus Nerve Vitality" is designed to demystify the vagus nerve's role. It's a key player in our body's ability to manage stress and maintain balance. Here, I share the somatic practices that have significantly improved my gut health, alleviated my stress, and reduced inflammation, which has been central to my healing process.

This book's approach is unique—it combines the rigors of scientific research with the simplicity of practical exercises and the intimacy of personal stories. Whether you are seated at a desk all day, an active individual facing physical strain, or a medical professional seeking to enrich your therapeutic practices, this book offers valuable insights and practical methods that can be integrated into everyday life.

Let me share a moment that encapsulates my journey's essence. One evening, after a particularly intense somatic breathing session, I felt a wave of relief so profound that it seemed as though years of built-up tension had dissolved. This experience was a turning point for me and illuminated the impact of nurturing our body's innate ability to heal.

As we move forward, I invite you to read and engage actively with the exercises and reflections provided. This book is set up to be your companion in a journey of exploration and healing. Whether you are dealing with chronic pain, digestive issues, or simply the stress of modern life, there is something here for you. Please note that while the practices outlined in this book are grounded in research and personal experience, they are not a substitute for professional medical advice. Always consult a healthcare professional before starting any new health regimen, especially if you have pre-existing health conditions.

I warmly invite you to join me on this path of discovery and healing. Together, let's explore our bodies' and minds' remarkable capabilities to create greater well-being and vitality.

CHAPTER 1: UNDERSTANDING THE VAGUS NERVE

Have you ever wondered why your heart races when you're frightened or why a deep breath can calm your nerves? These reactions are orchestrated by an unseen but incredibly influential part of your body called the vagus nerve. This nerve serves as a command center for managing your body's relaxation responses. Yet, it remains one of the most underappreciated aspects of our physiology. In this chapter, we will explore the essential functions and profound impact of the vagus nerve, shedding light on how it holds the key to balancing our physical, mental, and emotional health. Ready? Let's go!

WHAT IS THE VAGUS NERVE, AND WHY DOES IT MATTER?

The vagus (or vagal) nerve, known scientifically as the tenth cranial nerve, is a fundamental component of the autonomic nervous system, which controls our body's involuntary functions. This includes everything from modulating our heart rate to managing digestion and respiratory rates. The vagus nerve's uniqueness lies in its extensive reach—its fibers extend from the brainstem through the neck and chest down to the abdomen, making it the longest and most complex of the cranial nerves.

Biological Significance

The vagus nerve is a vital part of the autonomic nervous system and acts like a superhighway for signals between the brain and vital organs such as the heart, lungs, and digestive system. Think of it as a two-way communication system: the brain sends instructions, and the body responds with feedback. For example, if you're stressed, the vagus nerve helps lower your heart rate and promotes relaxation, essentially telling your body, "It's okay; you can calm down now." This ability to adapt and regulate is critical for maintaining homeostasis, which keeps your body's internal environment stable despite changes outside.

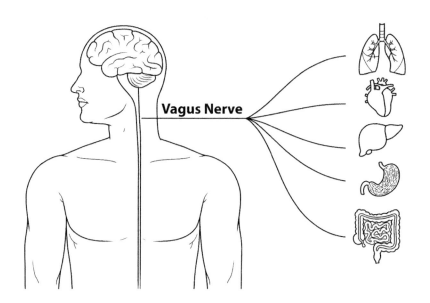

Health Implications

The vagus nerve's health is paramount, as its proper functioning is integral to our overall well-being. Its role is evident in a wide array of bodily functions and, consequently, in various health conditions. For example, an underactive vagus nerve can be linked to issues such as anxiety, heart disease, and chronic inflammation. On the flip side, stimulating the vagus nerve has been found to improve conditions like anxiety and depression, showcasing its capacity to influence our health profoundly. Essentially, a well-functioning vagus nerve acts as a keystone for bodily health, orchestrating multiple organ systems to work in harmony and respond effectively to stress.

Historical Context

The vagus nerve's significance has been acknowledged in medical texts for centuries. However, its comprehensive impact has only been widely recognized in recent decades. Ancient texts recognized the nerve for its role in voice and breathing. However, its broader physiological and psychological impacts were not well understood. As medical science advanced, researchers uncovered the vagus nerve's extensive influence on the autonomic nervous system. Significant milestones include discovering its role in the parasympathetic nervous system, which promotes relaxation and digestion. These discoveries have shifted the perception of the vagus nerve from a mere structural entity to a pivotal component in neurology and holistic health practices, highlighting its potential in therapeutic applications for a myriad of conditions.

Understanding the vagus nerve and its functionality is more than an academic pursuit; it's a major step toward achieving personal health sovereignty. By learning to regulate the functions influenced by the vagus nerve, you empower yourself to manage your stress responsively, improve your physical health, and enhance your emotional resilience. As we explore this remarkable nerve, remember that each piece of knowledge you gain is a tool in your toolkit for better health and well-being.

THE ANATOMY OF THE VAGUS NERVE: VISUAL GUIDES

The intricate neural network of the human body includes numerous nerves, but none quite as fascinating and extensive as the vagus nerve. Originating from the brainstem, this remarkable nerve branches downward, weaving through the neck and thorax and extending into the abdomen. It serves as a critical connector, sending numerous fibers to the heart, lungs, and digestive tract, among other organs. This widespread distribution highlights its importance and underscores its role in an array of essential bodily functions, from controlling heart rate to managing digestion.

Imagine the vagus nerve as a tree whose roots begin deep within the brainstem, branching out through the body with long limbs and finer twigs reaching into various organs. This visualization helps us understand the nerve's physical structure nerve and its functional significance. The body's natural "wiring system" carries an array of signals to and from the brain to various organ systems, enabling them to function in harmony. For anyone looking to understand their body's responses to various stimuli—like the relaxation you feel after deep breathing or the stomach-churning you experience during stress—grasping the vagus nerve's structure and functions will be revealing.

To enhance comprehension, detailed diagrams and images can be exceptionally helpful. Visual aids that map out the vagus nerve's course, illustrating its origin in the brainstem and its extensive branching throughout the body, serve as excellent maps for learners and practitioners. These visuals make the anatomical details more digestible and help us visualize how integral this nerve is in connecting different body parts. Moreover, for those who appreciate a hands-on learning experience, exploring digital 3D models online offers a tactile approach to understanding the vagus nerve's anatomy. Manipulating these models can provide a dynamic perspective of how the nerve moves and interacts within the body, making the learning process interactive and engaging. Here is a visual 3-D model found on YouTube: The vagus nerve #meded #anatomy #3dmodel (youtube.com)

The vagus nerve is distinct not only in its size and reach but also in its functionality. Unlike other nerves that might serve more localized functions, the vagus nerve operates on a broader scale, affecting systemic functions across the body. It's like comparing a major highway to smaller local roads; while local roads serve particular areas, the highway connects major cities and facilitates broader connectivity. This analogy helps underscore the vagus nerve's critical role in autonomic control—regulating activities your body handles automatically, like your heartbeat, breathing, and digestive processes.

You may wonder why you need to understand the vagus nerve's anatomy. Well, it gives one a deeper appreciation of how our bodies manage stress, maintain homeostasis, and ultimately, survive. By visualizing this nerve's course through the body and acknowledging its comparative significance, we can begin to appreciate the delicate balance our bodies maintain every moment of our lives. As you reflect on this information, consider the marvel of human anatomy and the intricate systems that operate within us, often without our conscious effort. This knowledge equips us to take better care of our bodies by recognizing the signals they give us. It is simply outstanding! We must listen to our bodies!

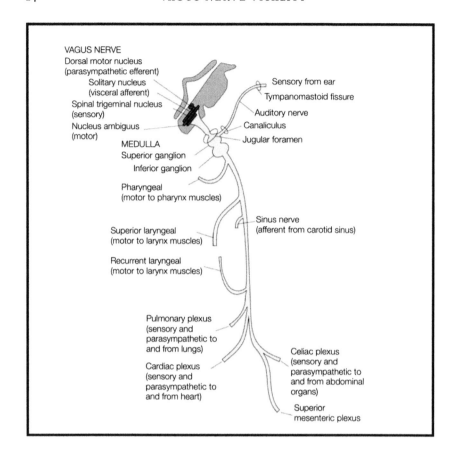

POLYVAGAL THEORY: UNDERSTANDING THE SCIENCE BEHIND IT

When Stephen Porges introduced the polyvagal theory (PVT) in 1994, it revolutionized our understanding of the autonomic nervous system, particularly the vagus nerve's role in emotional and physiological responses. This theory suggests that the vagus nerve has two distinct branches, each responsible for different behavioral responses to the environment. The ventral vagal complex, associated with the newer myelinated branch, supports social engagement and calm states. In contrast, the dorsal vagal complex, tied to the older, unmyelinated branch, triggers immobilization behaviors seen in responses to life-threatening situations. This view helps explain why our bodies react in certain ways under stress. For instance, when faced with a stressful event, a well-functioning ventral vagal system can effectively calm the heart rate and promote a feeling of calm. However, suppose the stress is perceived as severe. In that case, the older dorsal system might take over, leading to a freeze response—a state often observed in traumatic situations. This understanding provides a biological basis for behaviors previously thought to be purely psychological.

Evolutionary Perspective

From an evolutionary standpoint, PVT offers an intriguing explanation of how the human nervous system has adapted over millennia to meet our changing physiological needs. Originally, our distant ancestors only had the unmyelinated vagal system, which is still predominant in reptiles today, allowing for basic survival mechanisms like "playing dead" when threatened. As mammals evolved, especially social ones like humans, the myelinated system developed, enabling more sophisticated behaviors like social communication and bonding, which are vital for nurturing young and creating community bonds. This evolutionary shift from a primitive system focused solely on survival to one that facilitates complex social interactions illustrates how the vagus nerve's function is integral to our survival and social well-being. It underscores the importance of a balanced nervous system for individual health and the health of our relationships and communities.

Application in Therapy

In therapeutic settings, the insights from PVT have profound implications, especially in treating trauma and emotional dysregulation. Therapists trained in this approach often focus on strengthening the body's capacity to engage the newer, myelinated branch of the vagus nerve. Techniques such as deep breathing, social engagement, and even singing or chanting can help "tone" the vagal pathways, promoting feelings of safety and social connection that are often disrupted by trauma.

For example, consider a therapy session where a client learns to slow their breathing and engage in direct, warm eye contact with another person in a safe and structured environment. These actions can stimulate the vagus nerve system, signaling to the brain that the environment is safe, which helps mitigate the hyper-aroused state that's often seen in anxiety and post-traumatic stress disorder. This application of PVT helps clients manage symptoms and enables them to understand and influence their physiological states, giving them a sense of agency over their emotional lives.

Critiques and Current Research

While the polyvagal theory has been a groundbreaking addition to our understanding of the nervous system, it is not without its critics. Some researchers argue that the theory oversimplifies the neurophysiological mechanisms of the autonomic nervous system and calls for more empirical evidence to support some of its broader claims, particularly those related to the specific functions of the vagal pathways. Moreover, the application of this theory in clinical settings has been questioned regarding its efficacy and the extent to which it can be universally applied across different types of trauma and emotional disorders.

However, research continues to explore and often validate the vagus nerve's significance in emotional regulation and social behavior. Recent studies look into how vagal tone correlates with emotional resilience and recovery from stress, providing more nuanced insights into how these processes work. Advancements in technology that allow for more precise measurement of vagal activity are helping to clarify the relationships between vagal health, behavior, and psychological well-being.

Recognizing PVT's strengths and limitations helps us stay open to new information and cautious about applying scientific theories without sufficient evidence. However, the theory's value in enhancing our understanding of the body-mind connection and its application in therapeutic practices is undeniable. As we learn more about the vagus nerve and its significant impact on our health and behavior, we can better appreciate the complex relationship between our bodies and minds, leading to more effective strategies for healing and growth.

HOW VAGUS NERVE DYSFUNCTION AFFECTS THE BODY

When the vagus nerve's delicate balance is disrupted, the effects can ripple across multiple bodily systems, manifesting as various symptoms that might initially seem unrelated. Common signs of vagus nerve dysfunction include persistent digestive issues, fainting episodes, and irregular heartbeat. These symptoms can be perplexing and often leave individuals feeling frustrated with their body which seems to be malfunctioning without a clear reason. Imagine trying to send an important email in a place with a weak internet connection. Similarly, when the vagus nerve's function is impaired, the messages between the brain and body become intermittent and unreliable, leading to a range of physical disturbances.

The causes of vagus nerve dysfunction are as varied as the symptoms. Physical trauma to the neck or chest, for example, can directly damage the nerve. At the same time, an accumulation of chronic stress can indirectly disrupt its function by keeping the body in a prolonged state of heightened nervous system activity. Lifestyle factors such as poor dietary habits and insufficient physical activity can also contribute to vagal nerve dysfunction by negatively affecting the organs that the nerve interacts with, such as the heart and digestive tract. Again, we will compare it to a busy highway system; if one section is blocked or in disrepair, traffic snarls up, affecting the whole network. Similarly, when the vagus nerve is not functioning properly, it can lead to a traffic jam in your body's communication systems, causing significant health issues.

The impact of vagus nerve dysfunction extends across various bodily systems. For instance, in the digestive system, an underactive vagus nerve can lead to a slow emptying of the stomach, which causes bloating, discomfort, and changes in appetite. In the cardiovascular system, it might manifest as an irregular heartbeat or blood pressure fluctuations, which, if left unchecked, can lead to more serious conditions like heart disease. This interconnectedness underscores the importance of the vagus nerve in maintaining overall physical health and why its dysfunction can be so disruptive.

Preventative measures to support and maintain vagal tone help stave off these dysfunctions. Regular engagement in activities that activate the parasympathetic nervous system, such as deep breathing exercises, meditation, and gentle yoga, can significantly improve vagal nerve function. These activities work much like a tune-up for a car – they keep the nerve functioning smoothly, ensuring that it effectively regulates the body's systems. Dietary choices also play a big role in maintaining vagal health. For example, consuming a diet rich in probiotics can support gut health, thereby supporting vagal activity as a large portion of the nerve's fibers are located in the gut. Additionally, avoiding excessive alcohol and processed foods can help maintain overall nerve health.

Implementing these lifestyle changes can proactively enhance your body's resilience and reduce the likelihood of vagus nerve dysfunction. It just requires creating a daily routine with space for activities that help you relax and connect with your body. This might look like starting the day with a five-minute breathing exercise or ending it with a gentle yoga session. By regularly practicing these techniques, you improve your vagal tone and overall well-being, equipping your body to handle the stresses of everyday life better and reducing the risk of dysfunction.

Understanding the profound impact of the vagus nerve on your body's health systems highlights the importance of taking proactive steps to support its function. Through mindful attention to the health of this vital nerve, you can maintain a better balance in your body's internal communications and overall health, ensuring that each part functions cohesively. This holistic approach to health helps alleviate symptoms and supports a broader, more sustainable state of well-being.

THE CONNECTION BETWEEN THE VAGUS NERVE AND EMOTIONAL HEALTH

Understanding the intricate relationship between our physical state and emotions can be transformative, especially when considering the vagus nerve's role in emotional regulation and mood stability. Neurologically, the vagus nerve acts as a messenger, using neurotransmitters to communicate between the brain and the body. These chemical messengers help regulate heart rate, digestion, and, most notably, our mood and stress levels. In essence, when the vagus nerve functions optimally, it serves as a moderator, maintaining a balance in neurotransmitter levels and stabilizing our mood and emotional state. For instance, the neurotransmitter acetylcholine, released through vagus nerve activity, can decrease anxiety and promote feelings of calmness. This is why, after a deep, relaxing sigh, you often feel a sense of relief – your vagus nerve is working to calm your nervous system.

The concept of "vagal tone" refers to the nerve's activity level and health. A high vagal tone is associated with better emotional resilience and a greater ability to adapt to stress. A well-toned vagus nerve can efficiently regulate the heart rate and quickly control the body's response to stress. It's similar to having a well-trained athlete's heart, which beats slower but can promptly respond when needed. Individuals with a higher vagal tone generally experience lower rates of mood disorders, more stable emotions, and a higher overall sense of psychological well-being. In contrast, low vagal tone is often found in individuals experiencing depression and anxiety, suggesting a direct link between this nerve's health and emotional health.

Incorporating somatic practices like deep breathing exercises, yoga, and meditation into daily life can significantly enhance one's emotional health by stimulating the vagus nerve. These practices engage the parasympathetic nervous system, often referred to as the "rest and digest" system, of which the vagus nerve is a crucial part. For example, the practice of deep breathing helps in reducing immediate stress and strengthens the vagus nerve over time, enhancing emotional resilience. Similarly, yoga, with its emphasis on deep, mindful breathing combined with physical postures, stimulates the vagus nerve, helping to calm the mind and body. These activities support the body's natural processes of recovery and relaxation, making them extremely useful for maintaining emotional balance.

The efficacy of these practices is not just anecdotal; numerous case studies have demonstrated the positive impact of vagus nerve stimulation on emotional disorders. One notable example involves a patient who suffered from severe anxiety and could not find relief through medication or traditional therapy alone. After incorporating guided deep breathing techniques and gentle yoga into her routine, she experienced a significant reduction in her anxiety symptoms. Her heart rate variability, a key indicator of vagal tone, improved remarkably, illustrating how these practices directly enhanced her vagal health and emotional stability. This case is just one of many that highlight the potential of vagus nerve stimulation to transform emotional health.

As we explore the dynamic between the vagus nerve and our emotional well-being further, it will become clear that our bodies possess an incredible capacity to heal and regulate themselves. By understanding and tapping into this, we can unlock a more stable, balanced emotional state. Engaging regularly in practices that stimulate the vagus nerve fortifies our emotional resilience and enriches our overall quality of life. With each breath, stretch, or moment of mindfulness, we are nurturing our vagus nerve, empowering ourselves to face life's challenges with greater calm and clarity.

ASSESSING YOUR VAGAL TONE: A SELF-EVALUATION GUIDE

Understanding and assessing your vagal tone is an exercise in self-awareness and a fundamental component of maintaining and enhancing your overall health. High vagal tone is associated with better physical and emotional well-being, characterized by a better ability to regulate stress responses and maintain bodily functions. Conversely, low vagal tone can be linked to various health issues, including heart problems, poor digestion, and difficulties in managing stress and emotions.

One of the most reliable methods of assessing vagal tone and health is measuring heart rate variability (HRV). HRV refers to the variation in time between each heartbeat, governed largely by the autonomic nervous system. It is not the heart rate but the variation in intervals between beats. High HRV indicates a robust autonomic and vagal tone, reflecting the body's capacity to effectively adapt and respond to stress. Low HRV can indicate reduced adaptability and a potential strain on your overall health, often preceding physical or emotional health issues.

To measure HRV, various biofeedback tools are available, ranging from simple apps that use smartphone cameras to more advanced heart rate monitors that strap around your chest. These devices analyze your heart rate data to provide an HRV score, giving insights into your vagal tone and autonomic nervous system activity. Regular monitoring can help you understand how different activities, such as exercise, meditation, or changes in your routine, affect your vagal health.

In addition to using technological tools, you can perform simple self-assessment exercises to get a sense of your vagal tone. One simple test involves observing your body's response to deep, slow breathing. Sit quietly and take a deep breath in for about five seconds, then exhale slowly for another five seconds. Repeat this for a minute and pay attention to how your heart rate changes: your heart should slow down when you exhale and speed up when you inhale. This response, known as respiratory sinus arrhythmia, is a good indicator of vagal tone. A noticeable change in heart rate during this exercise suggests a healthier vagal tone.

Improving your vagal tone can benefit your health immensely; fortunately, several effective ways exist to enhance it. Regular engagement in activities that promote relaxation and reduce stress is beneficial. Practices such as yoga and meditation improve HRV and vagal tone by stimulating the "rest and digest" part of your autonomic nervous system. Simple daily habits like singing, humming, or even engaging in social activities can also stimulate the vagus nerve and enhance its tone.

Diet is also important in maintaining a healthy vagus nerve. Foods rich in probiotics, such as yogurt, kefir, and sauerkraut, can improve gut health and, by extension, vagal tone due to the extensive network of vagus nerve fibers located in the gut. Furthermore, ensuring that your diet is rich in omega-3 fatty acids, found in fish such as salmon and also in flaxseeds, can help combat inflammation, thereby supporting vagal function.

Incorporating some of these practices and habits into your daily routine can enhance your vagal tone, improving your health and resilience. Remember, the key is consistency and mindfulness—paying attention to how different activities and dietary choices affect your body and adjusting accordingly. Over time, as you continue to nurture your body's vagal health, you may notice significant improvements in your physical health and your emotional and psychological well-being.

CHAPTER 2: PRACTICAL SOMATIC EXERCISES FOR DAILY PRACTICE

I magine standing on the edge of a vast, peaceful landscape, breathing in the fresh air, each breath more refreshing than the last. This feeling of openness and calm isn't just a brief escape but a reminder of your body's incredible ability to heal and rejuvenate through something as simple as breathing. In this chapter, we'll explore breathing techniques that activate and stimulate the vagus nerve. They will in turn enhance your parasympathetic system—the part of your nervous system that promotes relaxation.

BREATHING TECHNIQUES FOR VAGAL STIMULATION

Deep Breathing Fundamentals

Deep breathing is simple yet profoundly impacts our nervous system. When you take deep, intentional breaths, you do more than fill your lungs with air; you signal your brain to calm down and take control. This simple act activates the vagus nerve, which in turn reduces your heart rate and lowers your blood pressure, ushering in a wave of relaxation across your body. The simplicity of this technique makes it accessible to everyone, regardless of their experience with somatic exercises.

Think of the vagus nerve as a muscle that can be toned and strengthened through exercise. Deep breathing is a workout for it. Just as lifting weights builds muscle strength, regular deep breathing enhances the vagus nerve's tone, making it more efficient and responsive. The mechanics of this process involve a fascinating interplay between your breathing patterns and heart rate variability (HRV), an indicator of your nervous system's health. High HRV means your body is better able to adapt to stress, while low HRV is associated with anxiety and fatigue. By engaging in deep breathing, you are boosting your body's resilience to stress.

Diaphragmatic Breathing

Diaphragmatic breathing, or belly breathing, is a technique that maximizes air intake and engages the diaphragm, the large muscle at the base of the lungs responsible for effective breathing. Here's how you can practice this technique:

1. Sit comfortably or lie flat on your back.
2. Place one hand on your belly just below the ribs and the other hand on your chest.
3. Breathe in deeply through your nose, allowing your belly to push your hand out. Your chest should not move.
4. Exhale through pursed lips as if whistling, feeling the hand on your belly go in and using it to push all the air out.
5. Repeat this breathing pattern several times, focusing on keeping a slow and steady rhythm.

This method helps with managing acute stress and contributes to long-term improvement in vagal tone. It's particularly effective in moments of immediate stress and can be used to restore calmness swiftly and efficiently. The immediate relief it provides should motivate you to make these techniques a part of your daily routine to help you manage stress effectively.

Rhythmic Breathing Variations

Beyond simple deep breathing, variations involving rhythmic patterns can have differential impacts on the body's stress response system. Two effective patterns are the 4-7-8 breathing and box breathing techniques:

- **4-7-8 Breathing**: This involves breathing in for 4 seconds, holding the breath for 7 seconds, and exhaling for 8 seconds. It helps control the pace of your breathing and increase the effectiveness of each breath.
- **Box Breathing**: Also known as square breathing, it involves inhaling, holding, exhaling, and holding again, each for an equal count of four. This technique is particularly beneficial in high-stress environments as it helps maintain focus and calmness.

These rhythmic breathing techniques enhance your nervous system's parasympathetic (calming) response by allowing more time for your lungs to exchange air, sending stronger calming signals through the vagus nerve. Incorporating these into your daily routine, especially in moments of stress or before challenging tasks, can significantly improve your mental clarity and emotional resilience.

Incorporating Breathing into Daily Activities

Integrating these breathing techniques into your daily life is simpler than you might think. Here are a few practical tips:

- **During Your Commute**: Use red lights or traffic jams as reminders to practice deep or rhythmic breathing. These techniques allow you to manage stress in various situations, giving you a sense of control over your stress levels. You can also practice rhythmic breathing while waiting in line at the grocery store.
- **Before Meals**: Take a few deep breaths before each meal. This helps digestion by activating the vagus nerve and sets a calm and mindful tone for your meal.
- **Preparation for Sleep**: Get comfortable in bed. Start with diaphragmatic or 4-7-8 breathing to transition your

body into a state of relaxation, making it easier to fall asleep.

By making these practices part of your daily routine, you'll enhance your vagal tone and enable yourself to get through the stresses of daily life more effectively. Each breath you take is a step towards a calmer, more centered version of yourself, enabling you to meet life's challenges with resilience and grace.

GENTLE YOGA POSES TO ACTIVATE THE VAGUS NERVE

The ancient art of yoga is more than just a series of stretches and poses; it is a profound interaction between mind and body that can significantly influence the intricate workings of the vagus nerve. We can engage and stimulate this nerve through specific yoga poses, promoting a sense of deep relaxation and stress relief that resonates throughout our entire being.

Imagine each yoga pose as a gentle whisper to your body, signaling it to unwind and release the day's tensions. Yes, yoga promotes physical relaxation but it also coaxes your nervous system into a state of tranquility and balance. For instance, poses that involve forward bends or those that open the chest encourage deep breathing, directly stimulating the vagus nerve. This stimulation signals your brain to lower heart rate and blood pressure, easing both mind and body into a more peaceful state.

Now, let's explore some poses known for their effectiveness in activating the vagus nerve.

The Cat-Cow stretch is a fluid movement between arching and rounding your back while positioned on your hands and knees. It warms the body, brings flexibility to the spine, and encourages deep, rhythmic breathing that enhances vagal activation.

Child's Pose, with its forward bend and relaxed breathing, serves as a sanctuary of comfort, allowing you to turn inward and calm your nervous system.

Legs-Up-the-Wall, a restorative pose where you lie on your back with your legs extended upward against a wall, is particularly effective in soothing nervous tension and improving circulation, making it easier for your heart to rest and reducing the burden on your vagus nerve.

Integrating these poses into daily practice doesn't require hours; a simple sequence performed consistently can yield significant benefits. Start with a few minutes of Cat-Cow to warm up your spine and sync your movement with your breath, creating a rhythm that massages your internal organs and activates your vagus nerve. Transition into Child's Pose, allowing your breath to deepen and your mind to quiet as you feel the comforting earth beneath you. Conclude with Legs-Up-the-Wall, letting gravity help with the venous return and allowing your heart rate to slow down, bathing your nervous system in calmness. This sequence will stimulate the vagus nerve and align your body and mind, preparing you for the challenges and opportunities of the day with renewed resilience and clarity.

We must understand that yoga is a personal and individual experience. Remember that each body is unique and has its own capabilities and limitations. Therefore, modifications and variations of these poses are helpful and necessary to make yoga accessible and beneficial for everyone. For instance, if holding the Child's Pose is uncomfortable, placing a cushion under your thighs can help reduce strain on your knees and hips, allowing you to relax deeply into the pose. In Cat-Cow, those with wrist discomfort can come onto fists or use yoga blocks to alleviate pressure. For Legs-Up-the-Wall, a bolster or pillow under your lower back can enhance the therapeutic effect of the pose and provide additional support.

By adapting these poses to meet your needs, you ensure that your yoga practice remains safe, enjoyable, and effective for nurturing your body and stimulating your vagus nerve. Whether you are a seasoned yoga practitioner or a curious newcomer, embracing these gentle poses can lead you to discover a more profound sense of peace and well-being that radiates from within.

GUIDED BODY SCANS FOR STRESS REDUCTION

Starting the practice of body scanning can be likened to turning the pages of a book written about you, by you, and for you. It's a journey through your physical sensations that often go unnoticed as you rush through life's busyness.

What is a body scan? It's a mindfulness exercise that involves mentally scanning yourself from head to toe, section by section, noting any physical sensations without judgment. This practice encourages you to inhabit your body more fully, tuning into the whispers and sometimes loud declarations of your physical form. Doing so helps reduce tension and brings about a state of mental calmness, making it valuable for those seeking relief from the clamor of everyday stress.

Simply lie down in a quiet, comfortable space and take the time to focus inwardly. Here's how you can engage in a body scan:

1. Begin by lying on your back with your legs extended and arms at your sides, palms facing upward. Close your eyes and take a few deep breaths to center yourself.
2. Focus your attention on the top of your head. Notice any sensations there—maybe there's a feeling of lightness or perhaps a slight tension. Acknowledge whatever you feel without trying to change it.
3. Gradually move your attention from one part of your body to the next—down to your forehead, cheeks, neck, and so on, right down to your toes. Spend a moment with each area, simply observing.
4. If your mind wanders or becomes caught up in thoughts about the day, gently redirect your focus back to the part of the body you last remember attending to.

5. As you scan down your body, visualize each part relaxing and releasing tension as you exhale. Imagine stress flowing out of you with each breath, leaving calm in its wake.

This process helps to ease physical tension and strengthen your mindfulness of present sensations. This awareness is key in recognizing how stress manifests in your body, often before you're even conscious of being stressed. The link between these physical sensations and emotional states is strong. For instance, tightness in the chest might accompany feelings of anxiety, while a clenched jaw might coincide with feelings of frustration or anger. By becoming more aware of these cues through regular body scan practices, you can better manage your emotional responses and maintain a clearer, more composed state of mind.

The mental health benefits of regular body scan practices are substantial. Studies have shown that mindfulness practices such as body scans can significantly reduce symptoms of anxiety and depression. This reduction is partly due to the way these practices enhance emotional awareness and regulation. By routinely checking in with your body and acknowledging your feelings without judgment, you develop a greater capacity to manage stress and can recover from emotional upheavals more quickly. This emotional agility is essential in maintaining mental health and creating a resilient spirit.

Incorporating body scans into your nightly routine can enhance your sleep quality, a big component of mental and physical health. To weave this practice into your bedtime ritual, simply reserve 10 to 15 minutes before you plan to sleep to perform a body scan. This practice signals to your body and mind, indicating that it's time to slow down and prepare for rest. Over time, this routine will become a cue for relaxation and should significantly enhance your sleep quality, leading to better health and more vibrant energy levels throughout your day.

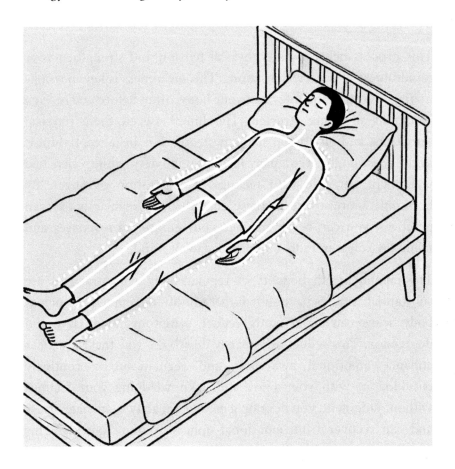

Through the gentle practice of body scanning, you grant yourself a space of calm and reflection where your mind can meet your body in a dialogue of sensation and awareness. This meeting's purpose is not to change what you find but to understand and accept it. This will create a foundation of mindfulness that will support all aspects of your life. Whether you're dealing with daily stressors or dealing with more intense emotions, body scans offer a pathway to deeper self-understanding and peace.

PROGRESSIVE MUSCLE RELAXATION FOR PAIN RELIEF

Our bodies are a little like finely tuned instruments, with each muscle capable of holding and releasing tension in response to the demands of our daily lives. When this instrument is tuned properly, it operates with grace and efficiency. Yet, sometimes, the strings—or in our case, muscles—can become overly tight, leading to discomfort and pain. Progressive muscle relaxation (PMR) is a technique designed to help you learn how to effectively release this tension in your muscles, layer by layer, leading to a deep sense of physical relaxation and pain relief.

The concept of PMR is rooted in the simple principle that physical relaxation can lead to mental calmness. Developed by Dr. Edmund Jacobson in the early 20th century, this technique involves tightening and then relaxing specific muscle groups in the body. This practice helps reduce physical ailments like muscle tension and headaches and also has a calming effect on the mind, reducing symptoms of anxiety and stress. By alternately tensing and relaxing your muscles, you increase your awareness of physical sensations, which can often go unnoticed under chronic stress. This heightened awareness can help you identify and address areas of tension before they lead to more severe pain or discomfort.

To practice PMR, find a quiet, comfortable place where you won't be disturbed. Start by focusing on your toes. Inhale and squeeze just your toes as tightly as you can for a count of eight. Feel the tension build, which may even be slightly uncomfortable. Then, as you exhale, release that tension, allowing your toes to become completely relaxed. Notice the warmth and lightness that follow the release. Next, move to your foot and repeat the process—tense on the inhale, hold, and release on the exhale. Gradually work your way up through each major muscle group in your body—

your calves, knees, thighs, abdomen, chest, arms, and up to your face and forehead.

As you practice this technique, you might notice areas where tension accumulates more frequently. This awareness is your body's way of communicating where it holds stress, allowing you to focus more attention and care on these areas. By regularly practicing PMR, you can learn to relax these muscles on cue, reducing the overall level of stress and discomfort you feel throughout the day.

The connection between muscle relaxation and pain management is well-documented. Tension and chronic stress can lead to inflammation, which exacerbates conditions like arthritis and fibromyalgia. By relaxing your muscles, you improve blood flow to these areas, which helps to flush out inflammatory cytokines and reduce swelling. This improved circulation can also accelerate healing by bringing more oxygen and nutrients to damaged tissues. Over time, regular PMR practice can help manage chronic pain and reduce your reliance on pain medication.

Incorporating PMR into your daily routine can have tremendous long-term benefits. For those who suffer from conditions like tension headaches, back pain, or even more systemic issues like hypertension, regular muscle relaxation can be a game-changer. The idea is to retrain your body's stress response, teaching it to respond with relaxation rather than increased tension. This shift improves physical health and enhances overall well-being and quality of life.

Consider making PMR a part of your evening routine, perhaps before bedtime, to help ease the transition into sleep. The relaxation induced by PMR can improve the quality of your sleep, providing your body with a better chance to repair and rejuvenate overnight. By dedicating just a few minutes each day to this practice, you should notice enhanced mental and physical health, paving the way for a more relaxed, pain-free existence.

INTEGRATING MINDFUL WALKING INTO YOUR ROUTINE

You can turn a simple daily activity like walking into a nourishing session of meditation and physical exercise. Mindful walking offers this transformation by making walking an intentional and enriching process. Unlike regular walking, where you move from one place to another without much thought, mindful walking encourages you to pay attention to every step, every breath, and every sensation in your body as you move. It's my favorite somatic exercise because it combines physical activity with mental clarity and relaxation, helping me become fully present in the moment.

To start mindful walking, begin with intention and awareness. Slow down your pace and notice how your body feels. Observe the transfer of weight from your heel to your toe with each step, the rhythm of your breathing, and the way your arms swing in coordination with your legs. Feel the contact of your soles with the ground and the textures underfoot, whether it's the smoothness of concrete or the softness of a dirt path. This heightened awareness anchors you in the present moment, turning a simple walk into a practice of mindfulness that takes your focus off daily worries and to-do lists. You might like to inhale for four steps and exhale for another four. This synchronization helps maintain a steady, rhythmic pace and enhances your focus and the meditative quality of your walk. The rhythmic pattern of breathing and walking harmonizes your body's movements with your respiratory system, creating a soothing, calming, and centering rhythm.

The benefits of integrating mindful walking into your routine stretch across both the mental and physical health spheres. On a physical level, walking is a gentle way to boost cardiovascular health, improve stamina, and enhance muscular flexibility. Practicing mindfully also increases your body awareness, helping you recognize and correct postures or gaits that may lead to discomfort or injury. Mentally, the practice of mindful walking is a good stress reliever. The meditative focus on breath and movement helps to quiet the mind and alleviate anxiety, providing a sense of peace and clarity that can carry over into other areas of your life.

Incorporating mindful walking into your daily schedule need not be a daunting task. It can be as simple as taking a ten-minute walk during your lunch break, using the time to step away from your desk and any screen-related activities. Let this time be a sacred pause in your day, a chance to reset and reconnect with yourself amid nature or even a quiet urban street.

Alternatively, you could start your day with a brief mindful walk instead of reaching for your phone. This can set a calm, centered tone for the day ahead. If evenings work better for you, a post-dinner mindful walk can be a delightful way to begin digesting your meal and unwinding before bedtime.

By weaving mindful walking into the fabric of your daily life, you'll create precious pockets of peace and restoration that will enhance your physical health and nourish your soul. Each step becomes a gesture of self-care, a pathway to greater peace and well-being. As you continue with this practice, the awareness and calm cultivated during your walks will begin to spill over into other moments of your day, enriching your life with a deeper sense of presence and mindfulness.

DYNAMIC STRETCHING EXERCISES FOR BUSY PROFESSIONALS

In today's fast-paced world, where many of us find ourselves tethered to our desks for hours on end, the importance of keeping our bodies active cannot be overstated. Dynamic stretching, which involves moving parts of your body and gradually increasing reach, speed of movement, or both, does not just enhance flexibility. It also improves blood flow, which is mandatory for those of us leading sedentary lifestyles. Think of your blood as a river nourishing everything it touches; better flow means more nourishment and less stagnation, translating to more energy and less fatigue.

Dynamic stretches are particularly beneficial because they engage multiple muscle groups simultaneously, mimicking the movements used in daily activities. This helps to warm up the muscles, making them more pliable and less prone to injuries, and stimulates the nervous system, heightening your mental alertness and physical readiness. For busy professionals who might not have the luxury of taking extended workout times at the gym, dynamic stretching offers a quick yet effective way to maintain mobility and reduce the risk of muscle strain.

Let's look at a simple, efficient, dynamic stretching routine that you can do in your office or at home (or your home office!). It will take no more than ten minutes. Start with leg swings: hold onto a stable surface for balance, such as the back of your chair, and swing one leg forward and backward. This movement stretches the hamstrings and hip flexors dynamically. Repeat this for the other leg.

Next, perform arm circles to loosen your shoulders and improve your range of motion. Gradually increase the size of the circles as you become more comfortable.

Follow up with torso twists—stand with feet hip-width apart and twist your upper body from side to side in a controlled manner. This helps loosen the lower back and waist area, regions commonly affected by prolonged sitting.

Transition into "open the gate, close the gate" exercises, which involve lifting your knee to a right angle and rotating it outwards, then reversing the movement. This exercise targets the hip area, increasing flexibility and mobility. Each of these exercises should be performed for about 30 seconds to one minute on each side, ensuring all movements are controlled and within a comfortable range.

The neck and shoulders are areas that often harbor significant tension, especially for those of us who spend long hours in front of computers. To address this, focus on stretches like neck rolls and shoulder shrugs. For the neck, gently tilt your head forward to stretch the back of the neck, then slowly roll from side to side, avoiding full circles to keep strain off the spine. For the shoulders, raise them towards your ears in a shrug, then release them down, feeling the tension melt away with each movement. These stretches can be particularly transformative, providing quick relief from the stiffness and discomfort built up over hours of stationary work. I practice these stretches daily as I sit for long periods in front of my computer. When my back, legs, or neck start to ache, I stop, take some breaths, do some shoulder and head rolls, practice leg lifts, and stretch my back.

You can easily incorporate these stretches into your daily routine during short breaks. For instance, take a few minutes to perform these stretches after completing a task or during a coffee break. This breaks the monotony of prolonged sitting and boosts circulation and flexibility. They'll help enhance your energy levels and productivity. When I have completed a task, I reward myself with some stretches and breathing exercises. It just takes making a conscious effort to include movement in your routine, transforming what might otherwise be a sedentary day into one filled with mindful movement intervals.

By incorporating dynamic stretching into your daily schedule, you actively contribute to your physical well-being, which in turn can enhance your professional performance. Regular practice of these exercises can lead to improved flexibility, reduced risk of injuries, and a better overall energy level, helping you to remain active and focused. Remember, each stretch serves as a moment of physical health enhancement and a valuable mental break, allowing you to return to your tasks refreshed.

This chapter has explored various practical exercises for you to add to your daily routine to enhance your physical and mental well-being. From breathing techniques and yoga poses to body scans, muscle relaxation, and dynamic stretching, each method offers unique benefits and can be tailored to fit your lifestyle and needs. As we move forward, we'll look at more specialized techniques designed to specifically target anxiety and stress, giving you resources to manage these common challenges effectively.

If you would like more information about somatic therapy and exercises for managing stress, anxiety, chronic pain, and fatigue, visit "Somatic Therapy for Beginners" on Amazon. It's packed with information about the mind-body connection and how to harness your body's wisdom to overcome emotional and physical challenges.

"Somatic Therapy for Beginners" is a comprehensive guide that builds upon the concepts introduced in "Vagus Nerve Vitality" by focusing more specifically on how our bodies store stress and trauma and how we can release this tension through therapeutic techniques. You'll learn about various somatic exercises that directly address the nervous system, helping to reduce chronic pain, alleviate anxiety, and restore a sense of calm and balance. These practices are designed to reconnect you with your body, enabling you to release built-up stress and restore physical and emotional well-being.

Whether you're dealing with physical pain, emotional distress, or simply seeking ways to improve your connection between mind and body, "Somatic Therapy for Beginners" offers practical tools and strategies to empower you on your healing journey. It's the perfect complement to the vagus nerve work you've already begun, offering a holistic approach to wellness that integrates body awareness, movement, and mindfulness. For more insights and actionable techniques, I invite you to continue your journey by exploring the transformative benefits of somatic therapy. Click the QR code to take you to "Somatic Therapy for Beginners."

Somatic Therapy

CHAPTER 3: SPECIALIZED TECHNIQUES FOR ANXIETY AND STRESS

In today's busy world, where life can get overwhelming, finding quick ways to manage stress is more important than ever. Imagine having a set of easy-to-use tools that can quickly calm your nervous system when anxiety hits. This chapter offers practical techniques that tap into the vagus nerve, helping you find instant relief from stress and anxiety.

QUICK STRESS-BUSTERS: VAGUS NERVE EDITION

Introduction to Quick Techniques

As we said before, the vagus nerve is a central part of your parasympathetic nervous system and helps regulate your body's response to stress. It acts like a brake pedal to your heart's racing engine in times of anxiety, helping restore a state of calm to your body.

Engaging this nerve through specific, fast-acting techniques can provide immediate relief from stress, effectively turning down the volume of your body's stress response like adjusting the dial on a radio. These techniques are designed to be quick and accessible, perfect for integrating into your busy life without stepping away from your daily activities. We will go into more detail about some of these in other chapters, as they're useful for more than just alleviating stress and anxiety.

Cold Water Immersion

Cold water immersion is one of the most refreshing ways to stimulate the vagus nerve. This can be as simple as splashing your face with cold water or taking a brief cold shower. The shock of cold water activates the vagus nerve, which sends a wave of calm throughout your body, decreasing your heart rate and blood pressure almost instantly. This method leverages the body's natural reaction to cold, which includes an immediate need to regulate internal temperature, thus activating the parasympathetic system —promoting calmness and relaxation. Washing my face with cold water before bed and when I wake up is one of my favorite ways to activate my vagus nerve daily.

Palming Technique

Another gentle yet profoundly soothing technique is the palming method, which involves covering your eyes with the palms of your hands. To practice this, rub your palms together until they feel warm, then gently cup them over your closed eyes. Allow your elbows to rest on a table or your knees to minimize strain. This simple action can shut out the world, giving your mind a much-needed pause from visual stimuli and soothing your eyes from the harsh glare of screens. The warmth from your palms helps relax the muscles around your eyes, calming your nervous system. This technique is particularly beneficial if you spend long hours in front of a computer or are overwhelmed by visual overload.

Scent Therapy

The power of smell to evoke memories and emotions is well-known. Still, scents can also be used to calm the mind quickly. Aromatherapy with calming scents like lavender, chamomile, or sandalwood can help activate the vagus nerve, encouraging relaxation. These scents stimulate smell receptors in the nose, which send calming signals directly to the brain, thereby reducing anxiety and stress. You can use scented candles, essential oils, or diffusers to surround yourself with these soothing aromas. Keeping a small vial of essential oil in your bag or at your desk can provide a quick and discreet way to access the calming power of scent therapy wherever you are.

Laughter as Medicine

Lastly, always appreciate the power of laughter for rapid stress relief. Laughter triggers the release of endorphins, the body's natural feel-good chemicals. It also stimulates the vagus nerve, contributing to a decrease in stress levels. Watching a short and funny video, reading a comic strip, or listening to a funny podcast are quick ways to introduce laughter into your day. These methods are sure to lighten your mood and shift your perspective, often providing the emotional distance needed to see stressful situations in a better light.

Incorporating these quick techniques into your daily routine can transform how you handle stress, providing immediate relief for your nervous system. Whether you have a minute to spare for some deep breathing, a moment for a laughter break, or even a few seconds to inhale a calming scent, each small step contributes towards managing stress effectively and living a more balanced life.

USING HUMMING AND SINGING TO CALM YOUR MIND

The simple acts of humming and singing are profoundly joyful and deeply rooted in our biological mechanisms for managing stress and enhancing well-being. When you hum or sing, the vibrations resonate in your sinuses and throat, engaging and stimulating the vagus nerve. The nerve responds to these vibrations by lowering your heart rate, decreasing your blood pressure, and soothing your anxiety. It's like tuning a musical instrument; humming and singing help tune your body, harmonizing your biological systems to bring about relaxation and reduce stress.

Let's explore a guided humming practice that you can incorporate into your daily life to help calm your mind. To begin, find a quiet place to sit comfortably without interruptions. Close your eyes to help turn your attention inward, and place your lips together while keeping your teeth slightly apart. Take a deep breath, and hum a single note at a comfortable pitch as you exhale. Feel the vibration in your chest, throat, and head as you sustain the note. Focus on the sensation of the sound waves moving through your body. Continue this for several breaths, experimenting with different pitches and noticing how the vibrations shift within you. This practice helps reduce immediate stress and improves vagal tone, enhancing your body's capacity to relax and cope.

Therapeutic singing involves choosing songs that enhance your mood and assist in stress reduction. The act of singing, especially songs that are calming or personally meaningful, can be incredibly therapeutic. Singing incorporates deep breathing, sustained notes, and expressive emotion, stimulating the vagus nerve. To integrate therapeutic singing into your life, create a playlist of songs that evoke a sense of peace and calm within you. Genres such as classical, soft jazz, or acoustic music often work well. However, the most important factor is personal resonance with the music. Play this playlist during moments of stress or when you need emotional uplift. Sing along softly or belt out the lyrics if you feel comfortable—let your intuition guide your voice.

Integrating music into daily routines can transform mundane activities into stress reduction and joy opportunities. Try humming or singing while you perform everyday tasks such as commuting to work or preparing meals. During your commute, for example, instead of focusing on traffic or delays, use this time to engage with your playlist, humming along to the melodies or singing softly. Humming and singing can turn a potentially stressful commute into a more pleasant and relaxing experience.

Similarly, play your calming playlist while cooking and sing along as you chop, stir, and season. This makes the task more enjoyable and infuses your mealtime with a sense of calm and satisfaction.

By incorporating these practices into your daily life, you actively enhance your mental and emotional well-being. Humming and singing are not just activities for entertainment; they are resources for transforming your mood and managing stress. Each note you hum or sing brings you closer to a state of harmony and balance, proving that sometimes, the simplest acts can profoundly affect our well-being.

THE ROLE OF GARGLING AND CHEWING IN RELIEVING ANXIETY

There are easy ways to calm down when your heart is racing during a stressful day. Gargling water and chewing gum are simple activities that can help reduce anxiety by using your throat and jaw muscles to stimulate the vagus nerve.

Gargling's Effect on the Vagus Nerve

Gargling regularly with water is a way to activate the vagus nerve, which can have a calming effect on your entire body. The mechanism is rooted in the physical act of gargling itself, which involves a series of muscle contractions in the back of your throat. These contractions are detected by the vagus nerve, which then responds by increasing its activity. Heightened activity of the vagus nerve helps to lower your heart rate and reduce stress, providing a quick and effective way to calm down when you feel overwhelmed. To incorporate this into your routine, try gargling with water after brushing your teeth, both in the morning and before bed. Practicing gargling helps maintain oral hygiene and ensures regular vagus nerve stimulation, aiding in stress management throughout the day.

Chewing as a Relaxation Technique

Chewing, especially gum or crunchy snacks, can help reduce anxiety. Your jaw muscles connect to the vagus nerve, so when you chew, they activate the nerve and help lower stress levels. This technique can be helpful in anxiety-inducing situations like public speaking or meeting tight deadlines. Keeping some sugar-free gum handy lets you use this technique anytime you feel stressed. Mint-flavored gum is a good choice because the mint can boost the calming effect.

Routine Integration

Integrating these practices into your daily life can help establish a routine that naturally reduces stress. Start your day in the morning with a minute of gargling after brushing your teeth. Gargling with water or mouthwash wakes you up and kick-starts the vagus nerve, setting a calm tone for the day ahead. In the evening, you might find that gargling before bed can help soothe you, making it easier to fall asleep. As for chewing, have gum or healthy crunchy snacks like carrots or apples handy when you feel anxiety creeping in. These can be particularly useful during your workday or when commuting, providing a simple yet effective tool to manage stress.

Scientific Evidence

The effectiveness of these techniques is backed by scientific research, which has shown that regular stimulation of the vagus nerve through activities like gargling and chewing can significantly reduce overall stress and anxiety levels. Studies indicate that these activities increase the vagal tone, which is a measure of how active the vagus nerve is in its role of calming the body. A higher vagal tone is associated with better emotional regulation and resilience against stress. By incorporating gargling and chewing into your daily routine, you are taking practical steps to manage stress and engaging in scientifically supported practices that enhance your body's natural ability to relax and maintain equilibrium.

CREATING A CALMING EVENING ROUTINE

The value of an evening routine in setting the tone for a restful night cannot be overstated. Just as the sun sets to signal the end of the day, a structured evening routine can signal to your body that it's time to wind down and prepare for sleep. Night routines help end the day on a relaxed, tranquil note, allowing you to disconnect from the day's stresses and recharge for the next. Engaging your vagus nerve through specific activities during this routine can enhance this effect, helping your body relax and rejuvenate.

Incorporate quiet pursuits like reading, journaling, or gentle stretching exercises into your evening routine. These activities keep you engaged in a quiet, reflective manner and gently stimulate your vagus nerve. For instance, spending time with a good book allows you to escape into another world, distancing yourself from the day's worries. Reading and focusing on the narrative can help decrease your heart rate and relax your muscles, signaling your vagus nerve that it's time to calm down.

Journaling offers a different escape by providing a space to download your thoughts and reflect on the day. This practice can be particularly therapeutic as it allows you to articulate feelings and thoughts that may be causing anxiety or stress. The physical act of writing can be a meditative process, engaging the vagus nerve and reducing stress. Additionally, ending your journaling session by jotting down things you are grateful for can shift your focus from stress to appreciation, further enhancing the calming effect.

Gentle stretching exercises before bed can also be incredibly beneficial both on a physical and mental level. These movements help release the physical tension that builds up over the day, which can often keep you from relaxing fully during sleep. Stretching engages the muscles and the breath, stimulating the vagus nerve and promoting a decrease in heart rate and blood pressure. This helps soothe the nervous system and prepare your body for a deep, restorative sleep.

ENVIRONMENT OPTIMIZATION

Creating a calming environment in your bedroom helps so much with getting a good night's sleep. The conditions under which you sleep greatly impact the quality of your rest, affecting everything from how quickly you fall asleep to how well you sleep through the night. Start with the lighting in your room. Dimming the lights or using lamps with warm tones an hour before bed can signal to your body that it's time to wind down, increasing your levels of melatonin, the sleep hormone. This simple adjustment helps ease the transition from wakefulness to sleep, making it easier to fall asleep.

Temperature and noise levels are also significant factors in creating a sleep-conducive environment. The ideal bedroom temperature for most people is around 65 degrees Fahrenheit (18 degrees Celsius). A room that's too hot or cold can interfere with your sleep quality, so adjusting your thermostat or using fans/heaters as needed can help maintain a comfortable sleeping environment. I set my thermostat to slowly raise the temperature to 70 degrees toward wake-up time to help keep cooling costs down. Regarding noise, a quiet space is essential for disturbance-free sleep. If you live in a noisy neighborhood or find it hard to block out sounds, try a white noise machine or earplugs to create a more serene atmosphere.

DIGITAL DETOX

In our digitally connected world, it's easy to spend the evening hours glued to screens, whether it's television, smartphones, or computers. However, the blue light emitted by these devices can interfere with your ability to sleep by inhibiting melatonin production. To enhance your sleep quality, adopt a digital detox by turning off all electronic devices at least an hour before bedtime. Instead of scrolling through social media or watching tense TV dramas, try listening to soothing music or an audiobook. You could read a physical book too! These alternatives can provide relaxation without the stimulating effects of screen time, helping your mind and body prepare for sleep.

Embracing these practices as part of your evening routine can significantly improve your sleep quality and overall well-being. By creating a structured routine that includes vagus nerve-stimulating activities, optimizing your sleeping environment, and disconnecting from digital devices, you set the stage for a night of deep, restorative sleep. This helps you recharge and ensures you are better equipped to face the next day's challenges with renewed energy and focus.

EMERGENCY ANXIETY RELIEF TECHNIQUES

When anxiety strikes suddenly and overwhelmingly, it can feel like a storm cloud has enveloped your day, and a cold hand has gripped your heart. In these moments, having some immediate, effective techniques at your disposal can be supportive and comforting. The following strategies are designed to quickly anchor you, providing a sense of control when anxiety tries to take the helm. One highly effective method is the 5-4-3-2-1 grounding technique, a simple mindfulness exercise that can help divert your mind from anxious thoughts and bring your awareness to the present moment. This technique involves acknowledging five things you can see around you: four things you can touch, three things you can hear, two things you can smell, and one thing you can taste. This process helps ground your senses, pulling your thoughts away from anxiety triggers and redirecting your focus to your immediate environment. It's a gentle reminder that you are here, in this moment, and not in the future scenario your anxiety is trying to draw you into.

Focused deep breathing also helps with managing sudden bursts of anxiety. Concentrating on your breath and controlling its pace, you engage the parasympathetic nervous system, which helps counteract the body's stress response. Here's a guided technique:

- Close your eyes.
- Inhale deeply through your nose for a count of four.
- Hold that breath for a count of seven.
- Exhale slowly through your mouth for a count of eight.

This breathing rhythm, known as the 4-7-8 technique, acts as a natural tranquilizer for the nervous system, slowing down your heart rate and inducing a state of calm. Practicing this at the first signs of anxiety can help prevent it from escalating and provide a sense of immediate relief.

Pressure Points

Understanding the body's pressure points offers a means of obtaining quick relief in anxious moments. One such point is the wrist. Applying gentle pressure to the spot on your wrist where you might check your pulse can stimulate the vagus nerve, which can help calm the body. In traditional healing practices, another practical pressure point is located between the eyebrows, known as the third eye point. Gently pressing this area for a few moments can help alleviate stress and improve emotional balance. These points are easy to access and can be stimulated discreetly, making them perfect for moments when you need a quick, calming intervention.

Visualization Techniques

Visualization is another remedy in your emergency anxiety relief kit. This technique involves picturing a serene environment or a calm scene in your mind's eye, effectively distracting your brain from distressing thoughts and focusing on peaceful imagery. Here's a simple visualization practice: Imagine yourself in a quiet forest, sunlight filtering through the leaves and the soft sound of a stream nearby. Picture yourself walking slowly, feeling the cool, mossy ground under your feet, hearing the gentle flow of water, seeing the dappled sunlight. This mental escape can provide a temporary refuge from anxiety, lowering your stress levels and bringing your nervous system back to equilibrium.

Portable Tools

Lastly, keeping small, portable items with you, such as stress balls or essential oil rollers, can offer immediate tactile and olfactory stimulation, which can be very soothing during a bout of anxiety. Squeezing a stress ball provides a physical outlet for nervous energy, helping to release tension. Essential oil rollers, particularly those with calming scents like lavender or sandalwood, can be applied to pulse points for a quick, soothing effect. These items are easy to carry in your purse or pocket, providing an on-the-go option to help manage anxiety wherever you are.

By incorporating these techniques and tools into your daily routine, you equip yourself with robust strategies to manage sudden anxiety effectively. Each method offers a unique way to quickly intervene, helping to restore your sense of calm and control when anxiety strikes. Whether you use them independently or in combination, they can significantly enhance your ability to navigate stressful situations, ensuring that stress does not derail your day.

DESIGNING A PERSONALIZED ANXIETY REDUCTION PLAN

Creating a personalized plan to reduce anxiety is much like cultivating a garden; it requires understanding the conditions that allow stress to flourish and carefully cultivating practices that restore balance and growth. The first step in this nurturing process is to identify what triggers your stress and anxiety. Begin by keeping a journal or using a digital app to track your daily activities, emotions, and the anxiety levels associated with each. Note patterns that emerge—perhaps your anxiety spikes with sudden deadlines at work, or social gatherings feel overwhelming. Recognizing these triggers will help you customize a strategy that directly addresses your stressors.

Once you have mapped out your triggers, the next step is to select techniques that resonate with your lifestyle and preferences. This is where the beauty of personalization comes into play—there is no one-size-fits-all solution. Consider the methods discussed in previous sections, such as deep breathing exercises, journaling, or even simple activities like gardening or painting that provide a meditative respite from the hustle of daily life. Choose activities that combat stress and bring you joy and rejuvenation. It's similar to choosing plants for your garden based on what grows best in your soil and climate but that you love—selecting stress-reduction techniques that fit your preferences will yield the best results.

Implementing these activities into your daily routine is the next step. This might seem challenging amidst a busy schedule, but consistency is necessary for effectiveness. Start small; perhaps integrate a five-minute meditation into your morning routine or a short walk after lunch. Gradually, as these activities become habits, they build a resilient structure in your day, like the trellis that supports climbing plants. Setting reminders on your phone or allocating specific times in your calendar will ensure you stick to your plan. Remember, the goal is to make these practices as routine as brushing your teeth—integral parts of your day that you wouldn't think of skipping.

Monitoring your progress will help you to understand what techniques work best for you and you can adjust your plan accordingly. This could be as simple as rating your anxiety levels daily and noting any improvements or setbacks. Over time, this data will reveal the most effective practices in reducing your anxiety and why. It's a process of trial and refinement, much like adjusting the amounts of sunlight or water for your plants until they thrive.

By following these steps—identifying triggers, selecting tailored activities, integrating them into your daily life, and monitoring your progress—you'll create a dynamic and effective plan to manage your anxiety. As we conclude this chapter, remember that managing anxiety is an ongoing process of understanding and adjustment. The tools and techniques provided are designed to help you cultivate a balanced, fulfilling life. Moving forward, we will explore how to extend these practices beyond personal management to seeking environments and nurturing relationships that support mental health and well-being.

CHAPTER 4: ENHANCING GUT HEALTH AND DIGESTION

Your body is fantastic. It is made up of systems that work together to keep you healthy. The vagus nerve plays a key role in these systems, especially in digestive health. It is so interesting to me how this nerve affects our daily comfort and nutrition. While researching this book, I learned a lot about gut health, and I can't wait to share with you the techniques and practices you can incorporate into your life to help with digestion and overall gut health. In this chapter, we'll look at how the vagus nerve influences digestion and helps maintain your body's balance, from the food you eat to the energy you use throughout the day.

THE VAGUS NERVE AND ITS ROLE IN DIGESTION

The vagus nerve, often dubbed the "wandering nerve" due to its extensive reach, plays a major role in the digestive process. It is like a power line that connects your brain to your gut, sending signals that orchestrate the release of enzymes and stomach acids essential for digestion. When you eat, the vagus nerve triggers the digestive tract to churn and move, ensuring that food is broken down properly and nutrients are absorbed efficiently. This nerve's ability to control muscle movements in the gut is akin to a conductor leading an orchestra, ensuring that each section comes in at the right time and harmony prevails.

However, just as a symphony can falter if the conductor is out of sync, digestive issues can arise if the vagus nerve's function is impaired. Symptoms of poor vagal tone—such as slow gastric emptying, where food remains in the stomach longer than it should, leading to bloating, discomfort, and other digestion problems—can be a sign that the nerve is not conducting as well as it should. Constipation, another common issue, can also result from this lack of effective nerve signaling, as the bowel movements slow down, causing discomfort and unease.

Your digestive system's efficiency doesn't just involve your comfort; it significantly impacts nutrient absorption. A well-functioning vagus nerve enhances the digestive tract's efficiency, aiding in the optimal absorption of nutrients from your food. This is important because no matter how nutritious your diet may be, the benefits are diminished if your body cannot effectively extract and utilize these nutrients. The vagus nerve ensures that your digestive system runs smoothly, maximizing the benefits of the foods you consume and contributing to your overall health and vitality.

The vagus nerve helps manage how your body signals hunger and fullness, influencing your eating behaviors and, subsequently, your weight management. It sends signals to your brain that regulate the sensations of hunger and satiety. An effectively functioning vagus nerve helps you feel fuller longer and can prevent overeating, which is often a hurdle in maintaining a healthy weight. Understanding and nurturing your vagus nerve's health is, therefore, a key component in achieving a balanced diet and healthy lifestyle.

Visualizing the Vagus Nerve's Influence on Digestion

To further illustrate the impact of the vagus nerve on your digestive health, consider this visual metaphor: envision your digestive system as a bustling city, and the vagus nerve as the network of traffic lights controlling the flow of vehicles (food) through the city (your digestive tract). When the traffic lights (vagus nerve signals) are functioning optimally, traffic moves smoothly, and there are no jams or delays—food is digested efficiently, nutrients are absorbed, and waste is managed effectively. However, if the traffic lights go haywire, you can imagine the chaos that ensues—similar disruptions occur in your digestive system when the vagus nerve's function is compromised.

This visualization underscores the importance of the vagus nerve in digestion and highlights why maintaining its health is so important for your overall digestive well-being. By keeping this "traffic system" in optimal condition, you ensure that your digestive health remains at its best, supporting your body's nutritional needs and contributing to your general health.

In the following sections, we will look more deeply at specific practices and lifestyle adjustments that can support and enhance your vagus nerve's function. I'll provide practical advice and easy-to-implement tips that will help you harness the full potential of this remarkable aspect of your anatomy. Whether you are struggling with digestive issues, looking to improve your nutritional health, or simply curious about how to enhance your bodily functions, understanding and supporting your vagus nerve can open up new avenues for health and vitality. Let's explore these strategies together, learning how to tune your body's orchestra to play the symphony of health in perfect harmony.

FOODS THAT NATURALLY STIMULATE THE VAGUS NERVE

Eating the right foods is important for your overall health, including supporting your vagus nerve. Certain foods can boost your vagus nerve's function, improving both your digestive and mental well-being.

Probiotics and Gut Health

The relationship between your gut flora and the vagus nerve is a fascinating dance of mutual influence and support. Probiotics, beneficial bacteria in foods like yogurt, kefir, and fermented vegetables, play a big part in this relationship. These microorganisms help maintain a healthy balance in your gut environment, essential for optimal digestion and nutrient absorption. When your gut flora thrives, it sends positive signals along the vagus nerve, enhancing its tone and functionality. This, in turn, improves the nerve's ability to manage digestion and stress responses. Integrating probiotic-rich foods into your diet doesn't just enhance your gut health; it also directly supports the nerve acting as a communication line between your gut and brain. Regularly consuming these foods can lead to noticeable improvements in how you feel, both physically and emotionally, as your body becomes better at managing stress and maintaining digestive health.

Omega-3 Fatty Acids

Omega-3 fatty acids, found abundantly in oily fish such as salmon and plant sources like flaxseeds, are well-known for their anti-inflammatory properties. However, their benefits extend beyond simple inflammation reduction. These fatty acids play a vital role in the vagus nerve's health by maintaining the fluidity of your cell membranes and facilitating the nerve's communication functions.

Incorporating omega-3-rich foods into your diet helps ensure that the vagus nerve can transmit signals effectively, which is essential for triggering the release of digestive enzymes and managing your heart rate. The anti-inflammatory action of omega-3s also protects the nerve's health from potential damage caused by chronic inflammation. This can be particularly beneficial if you're dealing with conditions like irritable bowel syndrome or heart disease, where vagal tone is needed for management and relief.

Antioxidant-Rich Foods

Antioxidants play a protective role in your body by neutralizing harmful free radicals that can damage cells, including those of the nervous system. Foods rich in antioxidants, such as berries, nuts, and green leafy vegetables, provide a defense mechanism that supports vagus nerve health. These nutrients safeguard the nerve's structure and function, ensuring it can effectively regulate your digestive and emotional health. Regular intake of these antioxidant-rich foods can help enhance your vagal resilience, making it more robust in handling stress and less susceptible to wear and tear from the body's metabolic processes.

Role of Dietary Fiber

Fiber, found in fruits, vegetables, and whole grains, is a well-documented cornerstone of digestive health. But did you know that its benefits also extend to the vagus nerve? Fiber enhances gut movement, which stimulates the vagus nerve, promoting the efficient movement of food through your digestive tract, including bowel movements. This stimulation maintains the vagus nerve's tone and health.

Additionally, a fiber-rich diet supports the growth of healthy gut bacteria, which interact with the vagus nerve to influence your mood and stress levels. By ensuring a regular dietary fiber intake, you keep your digestive system running smoothly and support your vagus nerve's optimal functioning, enhancing your overall well-being and stress resilience.

Each meal offers an opportunity to nourish this vital nerve, reinforcing its ability to sustain your health and well-being. As you continue to explore the impact of diet on your vagal health, remember that each choice you make can contribute to a more robust, more vibrant nervous system ready to support you in every aspect of your life.

SOMATIC EXERCISES FOR IMPROVED GUT HEALTH

In the gentle realm of self-care, the practices we adopt can resonate profoundly with our body's internal systems, particularly our digestive health. Somatic exercises, which emphasize body awareness through movement and breathing, are a nurturing way to enhance digestion and stimulate the vagus nerve, your body's intrinsic peacekeeper. Engaging in specific yoga poses, for instance, stretches and strengthens your body and massages your abdominal organs, promoting better gut health and encouraging the smooth operation of your digestive tract.

Consider the Peacock Pose (*Mayurasana*) and the Bow Pose (*Dhanurasana*), which specifically target the abdominal organs. The Peacock Pose, where you balance your body on your hands while extending your legs parallel to the ground, applies gentle pressure to the abdominal area. This pressure stimulates the digestive organs, aiding the breakdown and absorption of nutrients, and activates the vagus nerve, enhancing gut motility and enzyme secretion. Similarly, the Bow Pose, which involves lying on your stomach and bending the knees to reach the ankles with your hands, pulling your chest off the ground, offers a deep stretch to the entire digestive system. This pose improves blood flow to the digestive organs. It encourages the proper functioning of the vagus nerve, which, as we've seen, is necessary for maintaining an efficient digestive process.

Abdominal massages are another beneficial practice, serving as a direct method to encourage bowel movement and stimulate the vagus nerve. By gently massaging your abdomen in a clockwise direction, following the digestive tract's path, you help move the digestive contents along and relieve symptoms like gas and bloating. This physical stimulation of the gut area also activates the vagus nerve, promoting a relaxation response throughout the body and aiding digestion. Incorporating this simple massage into your daily routine, after a meal or during a moment of relaxation, can significantly enhance your digestive health and contribute to overall well-being.

Breathing exercises, particularly diaphragmatic breathing, further support digestive health by enhancing abdominal pressure, which can help stimulate gastrointestinal function. This type of breathing involves a deep inhalation that expands the diaphragm downward, increasing intra-abdominal pressure and stimulating the vagus nerve. As you exhale and the diaphragm contracts, the abdominal organs are compressed, which can help propel digested food through the intestines and promote regular bowel movements. Regular practice of diaphragmatic breathing not only aids in digestive efficiency but also reduces stress, which is often a contributing factor to digestive disorders.

Regular movement routines, even those as simple as a daily walk or light stretching, can significantly benefit your digestive system. Physical activity increases blood flow to the digestive tract, which helps muscles function more efficiently and enables your body to process food more effectively. Additionally, regular movement stimulates the vagus nerve, promoting a healthy digestive rhythm and reducing symptoms of digestive distress such as irregular bowel movements and indigestion. Integrating light, regular exercise into your routine is an enjoyable and effective way to maintain not only your digestive health but also your overall vitality.

Adopting these somatic practices offers a holistic approach to enhancing your digestive health, integrating physical movements, breathing techniques, and mindful awareness to nurture your body's digestive system and the vagus nerve. Each practice, from targeted yoga poses and abdominal massages to breathing exercises and regular physical activity, uniquely fosters a healthy, responsive digestive tract. Each step, stretch, and breath is an investment in your health, enhancing your body's natural ability to thrive and providing a foundation for lasting vitality.

MINDFUL EATING PRACTICES TO ENHANCE DIGESTION

Stepping into the world of mindful eating opens up a new perspective on how we interact with our food. What we eat is important but how we eat can significantly influence our digestion and overall health too. Mindful eating revolves around the concept of being fully present with each meal, engaging all senses to experience the act of eating with awareness and appreciation. This approach transforms the mealtime experience and stimulates the vagus nerve, enhancing the digestive process and contributing to emotional well-being.

To practice mindful eating, start by slowing down and removing distractions. This means turning off the TV, putting away your phone, and ensuring that you're seated comfortably at a table. As you take your first bite, focus on the textures and flavors of the food. Chew slowly, allowing yourself to truly taste each morsel. Notice the crunchiness of vegetables, the richness of nuts, or the sweetness of fruit. By chewing thoroughly, you make it easier for your digestive system to process food and give your brain time to register fullness, which can prevent overeating. Slowing down and savoring each bite can make meals more satisfying and enjoyable, reducing the likelihood of mindless snacking later.

The psychological benefits of this eating style are profound. Engaging in mindful eating practices regularly can help reduce stress and anxiety around food. This is particularly beneficial for those who may have a tumultuous relationship with eating or body image issues. By focusing on the present moment and the sensations associated with eating, you learn to appreciate food as a source of nourishment and pleasure rather than a cause for guilt or anxiety. This shift in perspective can lead to a healthier approach to food and improved mental health.

Creating a calming dining environment also enhances the mindful eating experience. Start by making your dining area visually appealing and relaxing. Use comfortable seating and add soothing background music or a centerpiece of fresh flowers. The goal is to make your dining space inviting and tranquil, where you can comfortably slow down and enjoy your meals. Implementing a routine where you set the table nicely, even if dining alone, reinforces the importance of mealtime as a special, mindful occasion.

Weekly Mindful Eating Plan

To help integrate mindful eating into your daily life, here's a simple and healthy meal plan for a week that encourages mindfulness and optimal digestion:

- Monday:
    - Breakfast: Oatmeal topped with blueberries and a dollop of yogurt
    - Lunch: Quinoa salad with chickpeas, cucumber, cherry tomatoes, and a lemon-tahini dressing
    - Dinner: Grilled salmon with a side of steamed broccoli and sweet potato
- Tuesday:
    - Breakfast: Green smoothie with spinach, banana, and almond milk
    - Lunch: Turkey and avocado wrap with whole grain tortilla and mixed greens
    - Dinner: Stir-fried tofu with bell peppers, broccoli, and teriyaki sauce over brown rice
- Wednesday:
    - Breakfast: Greek yogurt with sliced strawberries and a sprinkle of flaxseeds
    - Lunch: Lentil soup with a side of whole-grain bread
    - Dinner: Baked chicken breast with quinoa and steamed asparagus

- Thursday:
  - Breakfast: Scrambled eggs with spinach and mushrooms
  - Lunch: Mixed bean salad with olive oil and vinegar dressing
  - Dinner: Beef stir-fry with vegetables and a side of jasmine rice
- Friday:
  - Breakfast: Cottage cheese with sliced peaches and honey
  - Lunch: Baked falafel with hummus and tabbouleh
  - Dinner: Pasta with pesto sauce and sun-dried tomatoes topped with grilled chicken breast
- Saturday:
  - Breakfast: Pancakes topped with fresh berries and a small amount of maple syrup
  - Lunch: Grilled vegetable and goat cheese panini
  - Dinner: Shrimp and vegetable kebabs with a side of couscous
- Sunday:
  - Breakfast: French toast with a dusting of powdered sugar and slices of banana
  - Lunch: Caprese salad with fresh mozzarella, tomatoes, basil, and balsamic glaze
  - Dinner: Roast beef with roasted carrots, potatoes, and green beans

Each meal is designed to be nourishing and a delight to the senses, encouraging you to engage fully with the experience of eating. By following this plan, you can explore a variety of flavors and textures, enhancing your connection to your meals and promoting a healthier, more mindful approach to eating.

COMBATING BLOATING AND DISCOMFORT NATURALLY

Continuing with everyday life while suffering from the discomforts of bloating can feel like a daunting task. Bloating sometimes seems to arise from nowhere and it can be difficult to pinpoint its cause. Yet, understanding and embracing natural remedies can offer relief and a deeper harmony within your digestive system. Herbal remedies, for instance, have been used for centuries, harnessing the earth's gifts to soothe and heal. Peppermint, ginger, and chamomile stand out as beacons of relief in the natural health world. Peppermint oil capsules, for example, have been shown to significantly decrease the symptoms of IBS, including bloating, by relaxing the smooth muscles of your gut. With its refreshing essence, this herbal remedy acts like a gentle breeze that can clear away the clouds of discomfort in your abdomen.

With its warm, spicy undertones, ginger is a potent anti-inflammatory and carminative. It helps prevent the formation of excess gas and spurs its expulsion. Integrating ginger into your diet can be as simple as sipping ginger tea or incorporating fresh ginger into your meals. Its natural compounds stimulate saliva, bile, and gastric enzymes that aid in digestion, helping to ease the bloat and enhance your digestive comfort. Chamomile, too, is a wonderful digestive aid. Traditionally used to calm an upset stomach and relax the muscles of the upper digestive tract, chamomile tea can soothe the stomach and ease the digestive process, providing a gentle, comforting end to a meal or a peaceful end to a hectic day.

Hydration is also important in maintaining digestive health and combating bloating. Often overlooked, the simple act of drinking sufficient water is fundamental to the digestive process. Water facilitates the breakdown of food and absorption of nutrients and helps in the smooth passage of waste through your digestive system. Think of it as a river that carries away debris; without enough water, your digestive tract may become a dammed-up stream where waste accumulates, leading to bloating and discomfort. Consuming adequate daily water can help maintain this essential flow and support your body's natural digestive rhythms.

Sitting or standing also influences your digestive health more than you might realize. Proper posture during and after meals can significantly impact your body's ability to digest food efficiently. Slouching or lying down immediately after eating can compress your abdominal space, hindering the digestion process and leading to bloating and discomfort. By sitting upright, you give your stomach the room it needs to do its work effectively. After meals, taking a gentle walk can also help maintain an upright posture, supporting the natural transit of food through your digestive system. This simple habit of mindful posture enhances digestion and aligns your body for better overall health.

Addressing stress is another facet of managing bloating and digestive health. High stress levels can trigger the body's "fight or flight" response, diverting blood from the digestive system, slowing the digestive process, and leading to bloating and other gastrointestinal discomforts. Incorporating stress management techniques such as deep breathing exercises, yoga, or meditation can help reduce stress levels and support your digestive system. Deep breathing, as we've learned, activates the vagus nerve, which helps shift the body into a "rest and digest" state, promoting relaxation and allowing the digestive system to function more efficiently. This helps alleviate stress and minimizes the bloating associated with it, enhancing your ability to enjoy a comfortable, vibrant life.

By embracing these natural remedies and practices, you empower yourself with tools that alleviate bloating and enhance your digestive health and overall well-being. Each sip of herbal tea, each conscious breath, and each moment of mindfulness is a step towards a more balanced and contented life. As you continue to explore these natural solutions, remember that each small choice can make a big difference in how you feel, both inside and out.

THE GUT-BRAIN CONNECTION: WHAT YOU NEED TO KNOW

When we examine how our body systems work together, the gut-brain connection seems to be key to our emotional and physical health. This connection is a two-way communication network between the brain and the "second brain" in the gut, known as the enteric nervous system. What happens in your gut can affect your brain, and what your brain experiences can impact your gut. This relationship affects overall well-being and influences everything from your mood to your immune system.

Central to this communication network is the vagus nerve, which acts as a direct line between your brain and your digestive system. It's fascinating to consider how this nerve can transmit signals almost instantaneously. For instance, the very thought of eating can trigger the vagus nerve to signal your stomach to release acids in preparation for digestion. Similarly, when your gut is distressed, signals relayed through the vagus nerve can prompt emotional responses such as anxiety or stress. This highlights the vagus nerve's strategic function as a mediator in the gut-brain dialogue, ensuring that both systems work together to maintain your health.

The impact of emotional well-being on your digestive function is profound. Stress, anxiety, and depression can all manifest physically in your gut. This might include symptoms like nausea, stomach cramps, or diarrhea, which are common physical manifestations of stress or emotional upset. The vagus nerve is sensitive to emotional changes and can become less effective in regulating gut function during these times. This often leads to a slower or disrupted digestive process, affecting how well you digest and absorb nutrients. Conversely, a troubled gut can send signals to the brain through the vagus nerve, potentially leading to or worsening feelings of anxiety or depression, thus creating a cyclical impact that can be challenging to break.

To enhance the communication along the gut-brain axis, integrating therapeutic approaches like mindfulness and cognitive-behavioral therapy (CBT) can be significantly beneficial. Mindfulness practices help you maintain a moment-by-moment awareness of your thoughts, feelings, bodily sensations, and surrounding environment. This can be particularly effective in managing stress and reducing its impact on gut health. Regular mindfulness practices can help modulate the nervous system's response, enhancing the vagus nerve's ability to maintain a healthy gut-brain interaction. CBT, on the other hand, helps in modifying negative thoughts and behaviors associated with stress. By addressing these psychological factors, CBT can indirectly improve gastrointestinal symptoms by reducing the emotional distress that exacerbates these symptoms.

Incorporating these therapies into your routine will soothe symptoms and address the root causes of gut-brain miscommunications. Regular mindfulness exercises, such as guided meditations or mindful eating, can help recalibrate your stress response, reducing its impact on your digestive system. Similarly, CBT sessions with a qualified therapist can provide strategies to cope with anxiety and stress, improving your overall mental health and, consequently, your gut health. These therapeutic approaches will help you manage the delicate balance of your gut-brain axis, enhancing your ability to maintain both mental and physical health.

As we wrap up our exploration of the gut-brain connection, it's clear that this relationship plays an enormous role in our overall wellness. The interplay between our mental states and gut health is a vivid example of how interconnected our body's systems are. Understanding and nurturing this connection through targeted therapies and mindful practices can enhance your ability to manage stress, improve your digestive health, and create a greater sense of well-being. As we move forward, remember that each step you take toward understanding and supporting this connection contributes to a more balanced and healthy life, paving the way for continued exploration and growth in the subsequent chapters.

HEALING THE WIDER WORLD

"He who has health has hope. And he who has hope, has everything."

— THOMAS CARLYLE

When we're busy with the pressures of work and family life, it's easy to let all the small things that are bothering us physically carry on without taking the time to address them. Before we know it, we live in a permanent state of feeling a bit "off," and we forget that it's not supposed to feel that way. For me, I knew I was under a lot of stress, but the gut health issues and inflammation I was also dealing with had almost begun to feel normal. It was only when I started somatic therapy and felt things begin to shift that I really understood how much my stress was affecting me.

Your body has an innate capacity to heal itself, but it does require a little understanding and assistance, and I truly hope that the exercises in this book are helping you to bring your body back into balance. This is something I wish for everyone, and it concerns me how many people are under so much stress that it's taking a toll on their physical health in ways they may not even understand. Somatic therapy completely changed my life and my understanding of my body, and I feel that it's my calling now to share this information with as many people as I can. That's how it is that you come to be reading this book, and it's why I'd like to ask for your help now.

In order for this book to reach the readers who are looking for help, it's going to need to be visible when they're searching—and one thing that really helps with that is reviews. If you would be willing to take just a few minutes to leave your review online, you could play a pivotal role in helping someone else begin this transformative journey.

By leaving a review of this book on Amazon, you'll make it easier for new readers to find it and take the steps they need to take to dramatically improve their health.

Too many people are suffering unnecessarily, and together, we can change this. It may not seem like much, but a review is a powerful tool for sharing information, and your contribution is so valuable.

Thank you so much for your support. It makes a huge difference.

Scan the QR code below to leave your review on Amazon.

Scan me!

CHAPTER 5: ADDRESSING CHRONIC PAIN AND INFLAMMATION

Think of your body as a well-connected system where everything works together to keep you healthy. However, when this system gets out of balance, it can lead to discomfort and negatively impact your quality of life. Chronic pain and inflammation are common issues that many people deal with daily. In this chapter, we'll explore the critical role of the vagus nerve in managing inflammation and pain, providing new insights and hope for those looking for relief.

UNDERSTANDING THE LINK BETWEEN INFLAMMATION AND THE VAGUS NERVE

Biological Mechanisms

As stated in previous chapters, the vagus nerve is your body's superhighway of communication between the brain and many of your internal organs. It also helps with controlling the inflammatory response through what's known as the cholinergic anti-inflammatory pathway. This pathway is part of your body's internal medicine system—it can dampen inflammation when it spirals out of control, which can happen in various autoimmune and inflammatory diseases. When activated, the vagus nerve releases a neurotransmitter called acetylcholine, which binds to receptors on immune cells and signals them to decrease the production of inflammatory molecules called cytokines. It's a fascinating example of how your body strives to maintain balance and protect itself from harm.

Research Insights

Recent studies have shed light on how potently the vagus nerve regulates inflammation. Research published in renowned journals, such as *Nature*, has demonstrated that stimulating the vagus nerve can significantly reduce inflammation in the body. These studies have shown that electrical stimulation of the vagus nerve inhibits cytokine production and can dramatically alleviate symptoms in conditions like rheumatoid arthritis and inflammatory bowel disease. This groundbreaking research is paving the way for new treatments that target the nervous system instead of traditional methods that focus solely on the symptoms of inflammation.

Implications for Autoimmune Disorders

This research is significant for people with autoimmune disorders, where the immune system mistakenly attacks the body's tissues. Conditions like rheumatoid arthritis and inflammatory bowel disease involve chronic inflammation, causing pain and potentially leading to severe damage to joints and organs. Traditional treatments often include medications that suppress the immune system, but these can have serious side effects and don't always offer complete relief.

Vagus nerve stimulation presents a promising alternative. Targeting the body's natural inflammatory reflex provides a way to control inflammation at its source, potentially reducing the need for medication and improving quality of life.

We are just beginning to explore the potential of using the vagus nerve in treating chronic pain and inflammation. With the development of non-invasive vagus nerve stimulation devices, which can be used at home without surgery, this therapy could become widely accessible. These devices deliver electrical impulses to the vagus nerve through the skin, helping to manage pain and reduce inflammation. This treatment approach highlights the body's ability to heal and offers hope to millions worldwide suffering from chronic inflammatory conditions. It marks a shift towards addressing the root causes of these conditions rather than just managing symptoms.

For those suffering from autoimmune disorders, where the body's immune system mistakenly attacks its own tissues, the implications of this research are profound. Targeting the body's natural inflammatory reflex provides a way to control the inflammatory response at its source, potentially reducing dependency on medications and enhancing the quality of life.

In exploring the connection between the vagus nerve and inflammation, we uncover more than just the biological mechanisms at play—we discover a new realm of potential treatments that could transform lives. Understanding and ultimately taming chronic inflammation is complex and challenging. Still, we have a powerful ally in the vagus nerve. As we unravel the mysteries of this vital nerve, we open doors to innovative therapies that could significantly alleviate suffering and lead to better health outcomes for those affected by chronic inflammatory conditions.

SOMATIC PRACTICES TO REDUCE CHRONIC PAIN

Living with chronic pain can feel like carrying a heavy burden that only you can see and feel. It's a personal experience that can profoundly affect your emotional and physical well-being. However, gentle yet powerful somatic practices can help ease this burden by utilizing the body's own mechanisms for pain management, mainly through activating the vagus nerve. These techniques aim to reduce pain and enhance your overall sense of control and empowerment over your body.

Guided Relaxation Techniques

The most effective tools for managing chronic pain are guided relaxation techniques targeting the vagus nerve, such as guided imagery and autogenic training. These practices involve mental exercises that help shift your body into deep relaxation, thereby reducing the pain signals sent to the brain. For instance, guided imagery encourages you to envision a peaceful scene—perhaps a quiet beach or a serene forest. As you immerse yourself in this visualization, your body begins to reflect the calmness of the image, which in turn activates the vagus nerve's ability to lower heart rate and promote relaxation.

Autogenic training, on the other hand, focuses on repeating phrases internally that direct your body to relax and your mind to calm. Phrases such as "my arms are heavy and warm" cue your body to release tension. This process further engages the parasympathetic nervous system, of which the vagus nerve is a part.

Movement-Based Therapies

Gentle, restorative yoga poses and tai chi movements also help manage chronic pain by engaging the parasympathetic nervous system. These movement-based therapies incorporate fluid, mindful motions that help reduce muscle tension and promote blood flow, which are essential for healing and pain relief. Yoga poses like the Child's Pose or Pigeon Pose allow for gentle stretching of the muscles holding tension, offering relief and a sense of release. With its slow and graceful movements, Tai chi encourages a meditative state of mind that has been shown to decrease pain levels and enhance mental focus and emotional tranquility. Both practices encourage deeper breathing, which stimulates the vagus nerve and enhances its pain-relieving capabilities.

Manual Therapies

Manual therapies such as gentle massage and chiropractic adjustments can directly stimulate the vagus nerve, offering another avenue for pain relief. Massage therapy, especially techniques focusing on the neck and upper back where the vagus nerve is accessible, helps release endorphins, your body's natural painkillers. It also reduces muscle tension, alleviates nerve pressure, and improves organ function by enhancing blood circulation. Chiropractic care, meanwhile, aims to improve spinal alignment, which can help relieve stress on the nervous system and enhance the overall effectiveness of the vagus nerve in regulating the body's pain responses.

Breath-Based Exercises

Finally, breath-based exercises like *pranayama* offer a direct method to influence the vagus nerve's activity and, by extension, manage pain. *Pranayama* involves various breathing techniques that help control the breath and, consequently, the mind. Techniques such as the *Bhramari pranayama* (bee breath), where you make a humming sound on exhalation, directly stimulate the vagus nerve, promoting relaxation and pain relief. Regular practice of *pranayama* can lead to significant improvements in the way your body perceives and manages pain. By focusing on deep, rhythmic breathing, you encourage your body to relax and activate the healing potential of your parasympathetic nervous system.

Engaging in these somatic practices offers a holistic approach to managing chronic pain. They activate your body's natural pain-relief mechanisms, giving you a sense of control and well-being beyond mere symptom management. As you incorporate these techniques into your daily routine, you may find a reduction in pain and an enhanced quality of life, marked by greater ease and comfort in your body. These practices are not quick fixes but are part of a continuous commitment to your health and well-being, providing tools that support your body's natural abilities to heal and thrive.

NATURAL ANTI-INFLAMMATORY TECHNIQUES

In the quiet battle against chronic inflammation, the choices you make in your daily life are very important. Imagine your body as a garden—what you sow, you will reap. By incorporating anti-inflammatory foods and herbs into your diet, you are planting seeds of wellness that can naturally reduce inflammation's flames. Turmeric, for instance, is not only a spice that adds flavor to your dishes; the curcumin it contains has potent anti-inflammatory properties. Including turmeric in your meals, perhaps as a curry spice or as a comforting turmeric tea, can help manage inflammation effectively. Similarly, ginger is a potent anti-inflammatory agent known for its zesty flavor. Integrating ginger into your diet, whether as fresh slices in your morning tea or as a spice in your cooking, can aid in soothing inflamed tissues.

Omega-3 fatty acids found abundantly in foods like salmon, flaxseeds, and walnuts are another cornerstone of an anti-inflammatory diet. These fats are essential for your body and help to reduce inflammation. The science behind their benefit lies in their ability to produce resolvins and protectins, compounds that help end active inflammation in the body. To harness these benefits, aim to incorporate these omega-3-rich foods into your meals regularly, ensuring a proactive approach to managing inflammation through diet.

Shifting our focus from diet to daily practices, hydrotherapy, which involves water at varying temperatures, offers a unique method to stimulate the vagus nerve and manage inflammation. Alternating hot and cold showers can invigorate your body's innate healing mechanisms. The sudden exposure to cold water sends an electrical impulse to your brain from the nerve endings in your skin, which stimulates the vagus nerve. This stimulation can help reduce the production of pro-inflammatory cytokines. On the other hand, hot water can soothe sore muscles and improve circulation, aiding the removal of inflammatory byproducts from your system. This contrast therapy invigorates your nervous system and promotes a more profound sense of relaxation and well-being.

Quality sleep is another foundational pillar in managing inflammation. During sleep, your body goes into repair mode, addressing the wear and tear of the day and reducing inflammation. The link between sleep and inflammation is bi-directional; poor sleep can lead to increased inflammation, while increased inflammation can make it harder to get good quality sleep. Engaging in vagus nerve stimulation practices, such as deep breathing or gentle yoga before bed, can enhance your sleep quality by activating the parasympathetic nervous system, which helps you sink deeper into restful states. For me, deep breathing before bed, along with simple stretches, clears away the day and prepares me for a relaxing night. By prioritizing sleep and adopting practices that improve sleep quality, you are taking a step in reducing systemic inflammation and enhancing your overall health.

Lastly, managing stress effectively also helps to control inflammation. Chronic stress can trigger and exacerbate inflammatory responses in the body. Mindfulness meditation, a practice where you focus on being intensely aware of what you're sensing and feeling in the moment, without interpretation or judgment, can help manage stress by bringing about a state of calm and balance. Engaging in mindfulness meditation daily, even briefly, can significantly reduce stress-induced inflammatory responses in your body. This practice helps cultivate a mental state of peace. It supports your physical health by mitigating the effects of stress on your body.

By adopting these natural anti-inflammatory techniques— tailoring your diet, engaging in hydrotherapy, optimizing sleep, and managing stress—you support your body's natural defenses against inflammation. Each choice you make, from what you eat to how you manage stress and sleep, weaves a tapestry of health that supports managing inflammation and enhancing your overall well-being. You nurture your body's ability to heal and maintain balance through these practices, paving the way for a healthier, more vibrant life.

TAILORING EXERCISES FOR SPECIFIC PAIN POINTS

When managing chronic pain, the key to effectiveness often lies in personalization. Every person's pain is unique, not just in location but in how it affects daily life and emotional well-being. Understanding this, it becomes essential to tailor exercises and therapies to fit individual needs and pain points, ensuring that each approach alleviates pain and enhances overall quality of life. Customizing your approach to pain management requires a keen awareness of your body's responses and the areas where pain is most prevalent. Let's explore how you can adapt various exercises and integrate multiple therapeutic modalities to create a personalized pain management plan that addresses your unique needs.

Specific exercises can benefit those suffering from localized pain, such as in the lower back, neck, or joints. For instance, pelvic tilts and lumbar stretches work best for me when I have been sitting for long periods. These stretches can help relieve tension and strengthen the muscles that support your lower spine. Similarly, for neck pain, simple neck rolls or using a soft cervical pillow while resting can provide relief and help maintain proper alignment of your cervical spine. When dealing with joint pain, especially in areas like the knees or elbows, engaging in low-impact exercises such as swimming or cycling can improve joint mobility without placing excessive stress on them. Experiment and find what works for your body, being mindful of how different movements affect your pain levels.

Integrating different modalities can further enhance the effectiveness of your pain management routine. For example, combining heat therapy with gentle stretching can be particularly effective. Heat therapy, through warm towels, heating pads, or warm baths, helps relax and loosen stiff muscles and joints, making engaging in stretches that promote flexibility and pain relief easier. This combination helps in reducing immediate pain and aids in preventing future pain episodes by improving overall muscle and joint function. Similarly, incorporating relaxation techniques such as guided imagery or controlled breathing into your exercise routine can help reduce the psychological stress associated with chronic pain, making the physical exercises more effective.

Safety is paramount when engaging in any new exercise regimen, especially for individuals dealing with chronic pain. You must consult with your healthcare provider before starting new exercises or therapies. This consultation should include a thorough evaluation of your current health status and an assessment of any potential risks associated with specific exercises. Healthcare providers can offer valuable insights and recommendations tailored to your particular condition, ensuring that your exercise regimen addresses your pain effectively and avoids injury. They can guide you in gradually increasing the intensity of your exercises, advise you on pain management techniques, and monitor your progress, adjusting your plan as needed based on your body's responses.

By carefully tailoring exercises to your specific pain points, integrating multiple therapeutic modalities, and prioritizing safety and professional guidance, you can develop a personalized pain management plan that works for you. This approach aims to alleviate pain and by extension, enhances your capacity to enjoy life fully despite the challenges posed by chronic pain conditions.

THE IMPORTANCE OF CONSISTENCY IN PAIN MANAGEMENT

Living with chronic pain can sometimes feel like navigating an unpredictable storm. You may experience moments of calm followed by intense, overwhelming waves of discomfort. During these times, the power of a well-structured, consistent daily routine becomes your anchor, offering predictable relief and a framework within which you can find longer-term healing and improvement. Establishing a routine around managing your pain, especially one that involves regular vagus nerve stimulation, can transform an erratic ocean of pain into calmer waters.

A consistent routine provides your body and mind with a set of expectations and a healing rhythm. When you engage in regular practices, such as specific breathing exercises designed to stimulate the vagus nerve or gentle physical activities that keep your body flexible and engaged, you're not just easing the pain at that moment. You're also training your body to manage and anticipate pain more effectively, which can significantly improve how you experience and cope with pain over time. It's a process that will take effort at the start. However, with consistency, the practices will become part of your routine and you'll begin to experience progress and relief.

The benefits of such a routine extend beyond mere symptom management. Regularly stimulating the vagus nerve can enhance your body's natural pain relief responses and decrease inflammation. When regularly engaged, this nerve, a critical part of your body's relaxation system, helps maintain a more balanced internal environment, reducing the frequency and intensity of pain flare-ups.

However, maintaining motivation can be challenging, especially on days when pain seems relentless and relief feels minimal. Setting small, achievable goals is important during these times. Break down your larger objectives into manageable tasks. For example, if you aim to engage in 30 minutes of guided relaxation daily, start with five or ten-minute intervals and gradually increase the time as you become more comfortable. Celebrate each step forward, no matter how small. These milestones are your victories, and acknowledging them can provide the encouragement needed to continue. Additionally, keeping a pain diary can help you track your progress and the effectiveness of different strategies. It will also provide tangible proof of your journey, which can be incredibly motivating.

Adaptability is also important when managing chronic pain, as some days will differ. Adjusting your routines to accommodate how you feel on different days helps when your pain might be more intense; focusing on gentle stretching or breathing exercises rather than more active physical routines might be more practical. Listening to your body and being willing to modify your approach will help you maintain consistency without overtaxing yourself. This flexibility in your routine can make it sustainable over the long term, allowing you to manage your pain effectively while accommodating the natural ebb and flow of your physical and emotional state.

Consistency in your pain management routine doesn't involve rigidly sticking to a set of practices. Rather, you create a flexible framework that adapts to your needs and provides continuous support. Remember, each small, consistent step is a building block in your journey toward better health and reduced pain. Through regular practice, motivation, and adaptability, you can develop a pain management routine that addresses your symptoms and enhances your overall quality of life, allowing you to enjoy more of the moments that matter most.

ADVANCED TECHNIQUES FOR LONG-TERM RELIEF

Dealing with chronic pain can be exhausting. However, with the advent of cutting-edge technologies and innovative therapeutic approaches, new pain management horizons offer hope and relief. One such advancement is neurofeedback training, a technique that harnesses the power of brainwave patterns to teach the brain to manage pain better. Neurofeedback is based on the principle that by monitoring and responding to your brain's electrical activity, you can train it to modulate responses, including pain perception. This training involves attaching sensors to your scalp, which feed your brainwave patterns into a computer. The software then uses these inputs to create feedback—often a video or sound—that guides your brain toward more desirable patterns. Over time, neurofeedback can help reduce the intensity and frequency of pain by enhancing your brain's ability to regulate the body's pain response, fostering a sense of control and empowerment over your physical sensations.

Transitioning from brain-based techniques to direct nerve stimulation, vagus nerve stimulation (VNS) devices represent another frontier in pain management. These devices, which can be either implanted surgically or used externally, deliver mild electrical impulses to the vagus nerve. This stimulation helps modulate pain and reduce inflammation by activating the body's natural relaxation response. The beauty of VNS lies in its ability to provide continuous, controlled relief without the need for medications, which often come with side effects or potential dependencies. For individuals whose lives are marred by chronic pain, VNS devices offer a way to manage pain that integrates seamlessly into their lives, maintaining their functionality and quality of life.

For cases where pain is severe and persistent and less invasive methods have not provided sufficient relief, interventional procedures such as vagal nerve blockers offer a more direct approach. These procedures involve devices that block pain signals sent by the vagus nerve to the brain. While more invasive, these treatments can be life-altering for those who have not found relief through other means. The decision to pursue such treatments involves careful consideration and consultation with healthcare providers, weighing the potential benefits against the risks and invasiveness of the procedure. However, for many, the possibility of significant pain reduction is a worthwhile pursuit, offering a chance to reclaim a life curtailed by pain.

Alongside these advanced individual techniques, embracing a collaborative care approach can significantly enhance the effectiveness of pain management strategies. This model involves a team of specialists—including physicians, physical therapists, and mental health professionals—who work together to create a comprehensive, personalized pain management plan. This team-based approach ensures that all aspects of pain, both physical and psychological, are addressed. Physical therapists can tailor exercises and therapies to your needs, optimizing physical function and reducing pain. At the same time, mental health professionals can provide support for the emotional and psychological challenges that often accompany chronic pain, offering strategies to cope with anxiety, depression, and stress. By working collaboratively, these professionals can provide a holistic treatment plan that maximizes pain relief and enhances overall well-being.

In exploring advanced techniques for long-term relief, we see a landscape of pain management rich with possibility. From the brain-training capabilities of neurofeedback to the direct impact of vagus nerve stimulation devices and the comprehensive approach of collaborative care, these strategies represent the cutting edge of what's possible in pain management today. As we continue to push the boundaries of what's achievable, we open up new paths for relief and recovery, offering hope and support for those living with chronic pain.

CHAPTER 6: MIND-BODY THERAPIES FOR HOLISTIC HEALING

I magine stepping into a serene, sunlit room where every breath and movement brings you closer to understanding your body's subtle language. Here, amidst the quiet, a deeper dialogue between mind and body unfolds, revealing insights and relief. This sanctuary isn't a distant retreat—it's accessible through the integration of biofeedback with somatic exercises. This method harnesses modern technology to enhance the age-old wisdom of body awareness. This chapter invites you to explore how this powerful combination can amplify your body's natural healing capabilities, mainly focusing on the vital role of the vagus nerve in regulating bodily functions and reducing stress.

INTEGRATING BIOFEEDBACK WITH SOMATIC EXERCISES

What Is Biofeedback?

Biofeedback is a real-time technique that uses electronic monitoring devices to provide information about your physiological functions, such as heart rate, breathing, and muscle tension. You can learn to control these processes consciously by gaining awareness of them. The fundamental beauty of biofeedback lies in its ability to make you an active participant in your healing process. It demystifies the body's internal workings, offering you a visual or auditory representation of your physiological states. This immediate feedback creates a unique learning environment to experiment with different techniques to manage your body's responses.

For instance, when you monitor your heart rate variability (HRV) through a biofeedback device, you can see how deep breathing directly affects your heart rhythms. This visualization isn't just informative—it's empowering. You watch, learn, and adapt, gaining control over the autonomic functions once deemed involuntary. This process enhances your understanding of how stress and relaxation affect your body and allows you to actively influence these responses.

Combining with Somatic Exercises

Integrating biofeedback with somatic exercises, such as yoga or tai chi, enhances your ability to regulate the vagus nerve. Engaging in somatic exercises connected to biofeedback devices lets you observe how movements and breath work affect your body's stress indicators. This combination allows for a more targeted approach to vagal stimulation, enabling you to develop personalized strategies to activate your body's relaxation response.

For example, while performing a yoga pose designed to open the chest and stimulate breathing, biofeedback can show you how this pose affects your heart rate variability (HRV) or breathing patterns. This insight allows you to consciously adjust your posture or breathing to maximize the benefit on your vagus nerve, enhancing your overall calmness and well-being. Over time, this practice can improve your ability to manage stress and reduce anxiety as you learn to fine-tune your body's responses based on real-time data.

Tools and Technology

Several biofeedback devices and apps are available for personal use, making this technology accessible to anyone interested in exploring this method. Devices range from simple wearables monitoring heart rate and breathing to more sophisticated systems tracking muscle tension and brainwave patterns. When selecting a biofeedback device, consider what physiological functions you are most interested in monitoring and ensure the device provides accurate and real-time feedback.

Popular apps like Calm and Headspace offer modules that integrate biofeedback with guided breathing exercises, facilitating daily practice. These tools are highly user-friendly and designed to be incorporated into your daily routine, making regular practice achievable and enjoyable. Here are a few more biofeedback tools and apps that can help you track heart rate, breathing, and muscle tension:

1. **HeartMath Inner Balance:** This app, when paired with a sensor, helps you monitor your HRV and guides you through breathing exercises to reduce stress and improve emotional balance.

2. **Muse:** Muse is a brain-sensing headband that tracks your brain activity, heart rate, breathing, and body movements. It provides real-time feedback to help you improve your meditation and relaxation practices.

3. **Breathwrk:** This app offers guided breathing exercises and tracks breathing patterns. It can be used to reduce stress, improve focus, and enhance relaxation.

4. **Biofeedback Institute's Emwave2:** This handheld device monitors your heart rate variability and provides feedback to help you manage stress. It's portable and easy to track and improve your heart and breathing patterns.

5. **Core by Hyperice:** Core combines a handheld device with an app to guide you through meditation and breathing exercises. It tracks your heart rate and provides biofeedback to help you improve relaxation and reduce muscle tension.

Case Studies and Evidence

Numerous case studies and research findings support the effectiveness of combining expression with somatic exercises. For instance, a study involving patients with chronic anxiety showed significant reductions in anxiety levels after a 12-week program of yoga combined with HRV biofeedback. Another case study highlighted a patient with fibromyalgia, a condition characterized by widespread pain and fatigue, who experienced noticeable pain relief and improved sleep quality after using biofeedback while engaging in tailored somatic exercises.

These cases underscore the potential of biofeedback and somatic exercises as tools for immediate stress relief and as part of a comprehensive approach to long-term health and wellness. By providing a bridge between the scientific understanding of the body's functions and the intuitive wisdom of traditional healing practices, this integration opens up new avenues for personal health management and therapeutic interventions.

THE POWER OF VISUALIZATION AND MENTAL IMAGERY

Visualization, or mental imagery, is a practice where you use your imagination to evoke sensory perceptions. This technique is more than mere daydreaming; it is a focused exercise that engages your senses to create vivid and intentional images in your mind. The beauty of visualization lies in its ability to bridge the gap between the mind and body, harnessing the power of thought to influence physical and emotional well-being. By picturing a serene landscape or imagining a wave of calmness washing over you, you engage the brain's inherent ability to regulate stress responses and evoke feelings of peace.

The concept of mental imagery has been utilized in various therapeutic settings, including stress reduction, pain management, and performance enhancement. When you visualize, you activate similar brain regions when you experience the imagined activity. This process can stimulate the vagus nerve, crucial in controlling the body's relaxation response. One effective technique for vagal activation is to imagine a gentle wave of something warm – you can choose something like treacle, melted chocolate, or lava – flowing through your body, starting from the crown of your head and slowly moving downwards. This imagery promotes a sense of tranquility, physically relaxing the muscles, reducing heart rate, and enhancing vagal tone.

Visualization is also helpful for managing stress and anxiety. It allows you to construct a safe, peaceful place in your mind, accessible whenever real-world challenges feel overwhelming. For instance, if you're anxious about an upcoming presentation, you can visualize yourself delivering it confidently, with your audience engaged and responsive. This mental rehearsal can build your confidence and reduce performance anxiety. I use this visualizing process every time I am making a presentation. Similarly, during stressful periods, imagining a calm, quiet beach where you can hear the waves and feel the sand beneath your feet can provide a temporary escape, granting mental clarity and reducing physiological stress responses.

To cultivate a regular visualization practice, set aside a specific time each day, such as early morning or before bedtime, when you can sit quietly without interruption. Creating a conducive environment enhances the experience; a quiet room with comfortable seating and gentle, ambient music can facilitate more profound relaxation. Start with short sessions, about five to ten minutes each, and gradually increase the duration as you become more accustomed to the practice. Consistency is critical to reaping the full benefits, as regular practice can enhance your ability to control your focus and deepen your relaxation.

Incorporating visualization into your daily routine will surely enhance your health and well-being. Whether you use it to prepare for stressful events, manage chronic pain, or unwind at the end of the day, this practice provides a sanctuary of calm that can significantly improve your quality of life. As you continue to explore and apply this technique, your ability to handle stress will improve, your focus will sharpen, and your moments of relaxation become more profound, bringing serenity into your everyday life.

DEVELOPING A RESILIENCE TRAINING ROUTINE

Resilience involves more than merely bouncing back from adversity. It's about growing and thriving through challenges, transforming stress into an opportunity for personal development. The concept is intrinsically linked to vagal tone, as a well-toned vagus nerve supports a balanced emotional and physiological stress response. As we've seen, when your vagus nerve is actively engaged, it helps regulate your heart rate, calms your nervous system, and allows you to respond to stressors with greater stability. Thus, developing resilience directly enhances your vagal tone, which, in turn, fortifies your mental health.

A comprehensive resilience training routine incorporates several components designed to strengthen your capacity to handle life's inevitable ups and downs. Cognitive reframing, a vital element, involves changing your perspective on stressors, viewing them as challenges or opportunities rather than threats. This shift in perception can significantly reduce stress's psychological and physiological impacts. Stress management techniques like deep breathing and mindfulness help modulate your body's stress response. At the same time, emotional regulation skills help you manage and express your emotions in healthier ways. For instance, taking a walk before a difficult conversation can calm your mind and body.

Here is another excellent example: cognitive reframing can transform the anxiety of a job interview into an opportunity to showcase your skills and learn about a new organization. By shifting your perspective, the physical symptoms of stress—like a racing heart or sweaty palms—are mitigated, allowing you to present a more composed and confident demeanor. This positively affects the immediate situation and enhances your long-term ability to handle similar situations with less anxiety.

To build resilience, you can incorporate several exercises into your daily routine. One approach is to use challenge-response techniques, like setting small, manageable goals for stressful tasks. For example, break down a large project into smaller, more achievable steps and celebrate each success. Adaptive coping strategies, such as planning ahead and seeking support from others, can also help reduce the impact of stress. Regular physical activity is another effective method, as it naturally boosts endorphin levels and improves mood, helping you become more resilient to stress.

Incorporating resilience training into your daily life ensures that it becomes a sustainable part of your lifestyle rather than a sporadic effort. Start by identifying daily activities that typically trigger stress. Integrate mindful breathing into these moments, using your breath to anchor you in the present and reduce immediate stress responses. Regularly set aside time for reflection, through journaling or meditation, to process daily experiences and promote a deeper understanding of your emotional responses. This practice will help you recognize patterns that may be detrimental to your resilience and reinforce positive coping strategies in your routine.

Consider your morning routine an opportunity to set a resilient tone for the day! Engage in at least one activity that bolsters your mental fortitude, whether it's a physical workout, a few minutes of reading something inspirational, or a short meditation session. Likewise, end your day by disengaging from electronic devices at least an hour before sleep and unwinding with a relaxing activity, such as reading or listening to soothing music. When I changed from cable TV to a Fire Stick, I purposely did not add the device to the television in my bedroom. This allows me to achieve better sleep quality and ensures my day ends with a sense of calm and control.

THE ROLE OF MEDITATION IN VAGAL ACTIVATION

Meditation, often visualized as a serene practice reserved for monks or the spiritually enlightened, is an impactful tool that anyone can weave seamlessly into their daily lives to promote vagal tone. Various forms of meditation, particularly mindfulness and loving-kindness, have been shown to stimulate the vagus nerve, enhancing the activity of the calming parasympathetic nervous system. Meditating quiets down the fight or flight response and nurtures the rest and digest response, providing benefits from reduced heart rate and better digestion.

Mindfulness meditation encourages you to remain present and fully engaged with whatever you are experiencing. You might focus on your breath, the sounds around you, or your emotions. Paying close attention to these things helps calm your nervous system and brings a sense of peace with real physical benefits. Loving-kindness meditation, where you direct compassion toward yourself and others, can also be helpful. This practice reduces feelings of isolation and anxiety, strengthens your emotional resilience, and supports healthy vagal function.

If you are new to meditation, starting a practice can seem daunting. Here's a simple, structured way to begin:

- **Find a quiet space:** Choose a quiet spot where you won't be disturbed, preferably a corner of your bedroom, a comfortable chair, or even a place in your garden or local park.
- **Settle into a comfortable position:** You can sit on a chair with your feet flat on the floor, on a cushion cross-legged, or even lie down if that's more comfortable.
- **Focus on your breath:** Close your eyes and focus on your breathing. Notice the sensation of air entering and

leaving your nostrils or the rise and fall of your chest or belly.

- **Acknowledge wandering thoughts:** It's natural for your mind to wander. When you notice this happening, gently acknowledge it and bring your attention back to your breath. I once had a yoga instructor who told us to imagine the thoughts going through our minds during meditation as just a movie playing. Let them go and return to your breath.

Aim to practice for a few minutes each day, gradually increasing the duration as you get more comfortable with the process. Consistency is the main thing—even a short daily session is more beneficial than a more extended session now and again.

Research supports the profound impact of meditation on health, mainly through its ability to improve vagal tone. Studies have shown that regular meditation can increase HRV, reduce stress-related inflammatory responses, and even lower blood pressure, all indicative of robust vagal activity. For example, a 2018 study published in *Frontiers in Human Neuroscience* reported improve-ments in mood and gastrointestinal symptoms in participants who engaged in an 8-week mindfulness meditation program, under-lining the connection between mental practices and physical health.

However, starting and maintaining a consistent meditation prac-tice has its challenges. Common hurdles include finding time in a busy schedule, overcoming the frustration of not seeing immediate results, and managing the discipline of sitting still. Integrating meditation into your routine in small, manageable segments is helpful to ease you into it. Start with just five minutes in the morning, or include a few breathing exercises before meals. As for the physical discomfort of sitting, ensure that your meditation posture is sustainable and comfortable—use cushions or chairs as needed. Remember, meditation is a skill that improves with practice, not a performance that requires perfection.

By integrating meditation into your daily routine, you harness a powerful tool for enhancing your vagal tone and improving your overall health. This practice offers immediate benefits, such as a calm mind and a relaxed body, but also contributes to long-term wellness, helping you manage stress, reduce anxiety, and live a more balanced life.

AROMATHERAPY FOR AN ENHANCED MIND-BODY CONNECTION

Aromatherapy, the art of using essential oils for therapeutic benefit, is more than just enjoying pleasant scents. It can positively affect your physical, emotional, and mental health. As I write this chapter, I'm using peppermint and lavender oils in an essential oil diffuser in my office. Essential oils such as lavender, frankincense, and bergamot are known for their calming and uplifting properties and for their ability to influence the vagus nerve, enhancing your body's natural relaxation response. When you breathe in these scents, molecules interact with the olfactory nerves in the nose, which then send signals directly to the brain, affecting the limbic system, which controls emotions and influences the nervous system. Lavender, for instance, is renowned for decreasing heart rate and blood pressure, potentially increasing vagal activity and promoting calmness. I use lavender in my classroom for obvious reasons. Frankincense, on the other hand, helps deepen breathing and is often used to alleviate anxiety and depression, thereby supporting vagal function. With its light citrus scent, bergamot can uplift the spirit while soothing the nerves, making it particularly effective for balancing mood.

The methods of applying these essential oils vary, allowing for flexibility in integrating them into your daily routine. Diffusers are a popular method as they disperse minute oil particles into the air to create a calming environment in your home or office. This method is particularly effective during times of stress or when you seek to create a peaceful space for relaxation or meditation.

Topical application is another practical approach, where oils are diluted with a carrier oil such as jojoba or coconut oil and applied to the skin. This can be particularly soothing when oils are massaged into pressure points on the body, such as the wrists or behind the ears, directly stimulating the vagus nerve at accessible points.

Direct inhalation, where you breathe in the oil directly from the bottle or a few drops placed on a handkerchief, offers immediate benefits, making it a convenient option for quick relief from anxiety or stress on the go.

Creating your personalized blends of essential oils can be an enriching experience, allowing you to tailor the effects to your needs. For instance, a mix of lavender, chamomile, and cedarwood can be particularly beneficial if you struggle with sleep. Each oil brings its unique properties that synergistically promote relaxation and sleep. Start by selecting oils that address your specific health concerns and scents that you enjoy, as the pleasure derived from the aroma is an integral part of the therapy. Experiment with the ratios until you find a blend that resonates with your preferences and needs. Do remember that essential oils are potent, and a little goes a long way; often, only a few drops are needed to create a blend.

Approach aromatherapy with an awareness of safety and precautions, especially since essential oils are highly concentrated and can be potent. Always dilute essential oils with a carrier oil before applying them to the skin to prevent irritation. Be mindful of allergies and perform a patch test before extensively using a new oil. Moreover, some oils can be photosensitive, especially citrus oils like bergamot, making your skin more susceptible to sunburn. Ensure you are informed about the properties of each oil you use, and consult with a healthcare provider if you have any concerns, mainly if you are pregnant, nursing, or have a chronic health condition.

Aromatherapy offers a delightful and effective way to enhance your mind-body connection, providing a tool that promotes physical relaxation and uplifts your emotional state. By incorporating essential oils into your daily routine, you harness the power of nature's extracts to support your vagus nerve health, enhance your well-being, and transform your environment into a more soothing space. Whether through diffusion, topical application, or direct inhalation, the aromatherapy's benefits are vast. They can be tailored to meet your individual needs and preferences, enriching your journey toward holistic health.

CRAFTING A HOLISTIC EVENING ROUTINE FOR BETTER SLEEP

Setting up a holistic evening routine is beneficial and essential for your wellness. It prepares your mind and body for deep, restorative sleep. Engaging the vagus nerve through calming activities can significantly enhance your sleep quality, as this nerve activates the body's relaxation response.

One nurturing practice you can incorporate into your evening routine is journaling. This practice serves as a release valve for the day's pressures, offering a moment to reflect, dream, and sift through the myriad of accumulated thoughts and emotions. By transferring your thoughts from mind to paper, you clear mental clutter and engage in a meditative practice that quiets the mind and eases the body into a relaxed state. I cannot tell you how invaluable this can be, particularly when you are going through a life change such as divorce or menopause. This process, mainly done by hand, can stimulate the vagus nerve through the rhythmic motion of writing, encouraging a shift from the day's stress to evening serenity.

Gentle stretching is another element that can be seamlessly woven into your nightly routine. Unlike vigorous exercise, which can be stimulating, gentle stretching eases muscle tension without elevating the heart rate. Consider stretches that focus on the neck, shoulders, and back—which often harbor tension from daily activities. These stretches alleviate physical discomfort and signal the nervous system to shift into a lower gear, further enhancing vagal activity and preparing your body for sleep.

Listening to soothing music can also profoundly affect your vagal tone. The slow, melodic sounds help regulate your heartbeat and breathing, synchronizing your body's rhythms to more tranquil vibrations. Creating a playlist of soft, ambient tunes devoid of jarring transitions can be a therapeutic addition to your evening, enveloping your space in sounds that coax your mind into releasing the day's stress.

Environment Preparation

Your sleep environment can significantly influence the quality of your rest. This might seem like common sense, but a few small adjustments go a long way. To optimize your sleep environment, start with the lighting. Dimming the lights in your home an hour before bed can help increase melatonin production, the hormone responsible for regulating sleep. Use soft, warm bulbs in lamps or candles rather than harsh overhead lights to create a calm, cozy atmosphere that encourages drowsiness.

Temperature also plays a critical role in how well you sleep. The ideal bedroom temperature for most people is around 65 degrees Fahrenheit (18 degrees Celsius). This cooler environment helps decrease your core body temperature, a signal to your body that it's time to sleep. I set a timer on my thermostat so the temperature rises before I wake, helping to keep the energy costs down. In winter, I may sleep with the window cracked for cold air and ventilation. Ensure that your bedding and sleepwear are comfortable and appropriate for the temperature, adding or removing layers as needed.

Noise control is another factor to control. If external sounds such as traffic or noisy neighbors disrupt your sleep, consider using a white noise machine or a fan to drown out the disturbances. Alternatively, earplugs can be a simple yet effective solution for maintaining a quiet sleep environment.

Evaluating Sleep Quality

Understanding and improving your sleep quality requires paying attention to your feelings upon waking. Are you refreshed and ready to start your day, or do you feel groggy and sleepy? Reflecting on your sleep patterns can help you identify areas for improvement in your evening routine. For instance, if you notice that you frequently wake during the night, you might need to adjust your sleeping environment or evening activities.

Keeping a sleep diary can be an insightful method for tracking factors that affect your sleep quality. Note your bedtime, how long it takes to fall asleep, any awakenings during the night, and how you feel in the morning. Perhaps alcohol or caffeine beverages are having an effect. Over time, patterns will emerge that can guide you in fine-tuning your evening routine and activities to support your sleep.

By thoughtfully crafting a holistic evening routine, you engage in a practice of self-care that honors your body's need for rest and rejuvenation Each element of this routine—from journaling and gentle stretching to creating the ideal sleep environment—works synergistically to soothe your nervous system, enhance vagal tone, and prepare you for a night of deep, restorative sleep As you consistently engage in these practices, you may find your nights transformed into a peaceful respite, nurturing your body and soul in preparation for the vibrant days ahead.

As we conclude this chapter on crafting a holistic evening routine, remember that each small step to unwind and prepare for sleep can significantly impact your overall health. These practices encourage better sleep and create a deeper connection with your body's natural rhythms, enhancing your ability to thrive in your daily life. The next chapter will explore further strategies to nurture your body and mind, continuing our journey toward holistic health with the help of the vagus nerve.

BONUS PLAN!

Introducing the 28-Day Vagus Nerve Stimulation Plan, a special bonus gift for my dedicated readers! This carefully designed plan offers a comprehensive, step-by-step guide to help you success-fully stimulate and support your vagus nerve, allowing you to benefit fully from the techniques shared in my book. In 28 days, you will incorporate various practices, exercises, and nourishing meals that aim to optimize vagal tone, reduce stress, improve digestion, and enhance overall well-being.

The plan is divided into two sections to help you integrate these practices into your daily routine:

Daily Techniques and Exercises: Each day, you'll engage in simple yet powerful exercises like deep breathing, cold exposure, humming, and gentle yoga movements that are proven to activate the vagus nerve. These techniques are designed to fit seamlessly into your busy schedule and can be done at home, ensuring that you're consistently working to strengthen your mind-body connection.

Nourishing Meals and Snacks: A key component of this 28-day plan is a thoughtfully curated meal guide filled with vagus nerve-supporting foods. You'll enjoy nutrient-rich recipes that are anti-inflammatory and gut-friendly, incorporating ingredients like omega-3-rich fish, fermented foods, leafy greens, and magnesium-packed snacks. These foods are delicious and essential in boosting your body's natural ability to stimulate the vagus nerve.

This bonus 28-day plan is my gift to you—a practical, easy-to-follow roadmap that supports your success in stimulating the vagus nerve and achieving lasting health and wellness benefits. Let this be the jumpstart you need to experience profound positive changes in your mind, body, and spirit! Just scan the QR code to start your 28-day plan.

Bonus 28-Day Plan!

CHAPTER 7: FOR THE PROFESSIONALS: INCORPORATING VAGUS NERVE PRACTICES

Welcome to a realm where the convergence of neurology and therapy illuminates new pathways for healing and wellness. In this chapter, we will explore the transformative potential of vagus nerve stimulation (VNS) in clinical settings. On this frontier, science meets the subtle art of patient care. As health professionals, you are not just practitioners but also pioneers at the forefront of adopting innovative treatments that offer hope and relief to those enduring chronic conditions like epilepsy, depression, and pain.

VAGUS NERVE STIMULATION IN CLINICAL SETTINGS

Overview of Clinical Applications

Vagus nerve stimulation has carved a niche in the medical field, primarily due to its significant impact on conditions often resistant to conventional treatments. Traditionally, VNS has been a beacon of hope for individuals with epilepsy, offering a way to reduce seizure frequency and intensity when medications fail to provide adequate control. The scope of VNS extends into the realm of depression, where it's characterized by its unique ability to alleviate symptoms in patients who do not respond to standard antidepressant therapies. Moreover, its application in pain management is gaining momentum, with evidence suggesting that VNS can diminish the severity of pain experienced in chronic conditions, thereby improving patients' quality of life.

VNS involves delivering electrical impulses to the vagus nerve via a device implanted in the chest. These impulses then travel along the nerve into the brain, modulating neurotransmitters and neural circuits associated with mood, pain perception, and seizure activity. It's a profound reminder of how deeply interconnected our body systems are and how modulating one key nerve can radiate healing effects across various functions.

Techniques and Devices

Vagus nerve stimulation employs implantable and non-implantable devices, each serving distinct patient needs and conditions. The most common form is the surgically implanted device, similar in size to a pacemaker, typically placed under the skin in the chest. Wires from this device are then connected to the left vagus nerve through a small incision in the neck. For those seeking less invasive options, external devices can stimulate the vagus nerve through the skin, specifically targeting its outer branches in the neck or ear.

Choosing between these devices involves carefully considering the patient's medical condition, lifestyle, and the specific outcomes they hope to achieve through VNS. Each device type has its protocols for usage, with implantable devices generally requiring periodic adjustments to optimize their therapeutic effects. These adjustments are typically performed during follow-up visits, where the device settings are fine-tuned based on the patient's response to the treatment.

Procedure and Patient Selection

Selecting suitable candidates for vagus nerve stimulation is a meticulous process that thoroughly evaluates the patient's medical history, current health status, and the specific nature of their condition. Ideal candidates are typically those who have not responded adequately to conventional treatments and are seeking alternative options to manage their symptoms. The procedure for implanting a VNS device is considered minimally invasive. Still, precise execution is required to ensure the electrodes are correctly positioned around the vagus nerve.

Post-implantation, patients are closely monitored to assess their response to the treatment. Initial adjustments to the device settings are often necessary to find the optimal balance that maximizes benefits while minimizing potential side effects. This period sets the groundwork for effective long-term treatment.

Monitoring and Adjustments

Ongoing vagus nerve stimulation therapy monitoring is vital to achieving sustained therapeutic success. Regular follow-up appointments allow healthcare providers to assess the patient's progress and make necessary adjustments to the device settings. Monitoring techniques often involve evaluating symptom frequency and intensity and using diagnostic tools like heart rate variability to gauge the treatment's physiological impacts.

Adjustments to the device may be required to address any side effects or to enhance the therapy's effectiveness as the patient's condition evolves. This adaptive approach ensures that VNS therapy remains responsive to the patient's needs, offering tailored treatment that changes with their health journey.

Incorporating VNS into clinical practice expands the therapeutic arsenal available to healthcare professionals. It offers patients a lifeline when other treatments have fallen short. By understanding and utilizing this advanced therapy, you can significantly impact the lives of those suffering from some of the most challenging medical conditions, ultimately guiding them toward a path of recovery and improved quality of life. As we continue to explore and understand the full capabilities of vagus nerve stimulation, its role in transforming patient care becomes ever more apparent, marking a new era in medical science.

EDUCATING PATIENTS ON THE IMPORTANCE OF THE VAGUS NERVE

When you sit across from a patient, aware of the profound impact that understanding their own body can have on their health journey, the conversation about the vagus nerve becomes educational and potentially transformative. Communicating the significance of this nerve in everyday terms can bridge the gap between complex physiological concepts and practical, daily health practices. This communication translates a technical manual into a user-friendly guide for optimal body function. You need to bring the profound science of the body's "natural caretaker" into the light, making it accessible and actionable for those in your care.

Use relatable analogies to convey the vagus nerve's role, explaining how it regulates everything from heart rate to digestion and mood. For instance, liken the nerve to a power cable that connects and powers major organs, ensuring they work in harmony. When explaining how it works, you might say, "Just as a thermostat regulates your home's temperature, the vagus nerve helps regulate your body's internal environment." This approach demystifies the nerve's function and highlights its relevance in a way that is easy to grasp and remember.

Providing educational materials can further enhance understanding and retention of this information. Brochures that outline the vagus nerve's role in simple diagrams and everyday language can be immensely helpful. Videos, particularly animated ones that show how the vagus nerve interacts with different body parts, can also be engaging teaching tools. These resources should be available during consultations and as take-home materials for patients to study. Encourage them to bring any further questions to future discussions.

Incorporating discussions about the vagus nerve into patient consultations can be particularly effective when tailored to the individual's conditions. For someone dealing with anxiety or depression, explain how the vagus nerve influences neurotransmitter levels that affect mood and stress responses. For patients suffering from gastrointestinal issues, discuss how vagal nerve health could improve their digestive function. This targeted approach makes the information more relevant and actionable, as patients can see a direct connection between their issues and how enhancing vagal tone might help.

Lastly, the education process is always balanced. Gathering feedback from your patients about their understanding and concerns regarding the vagus nerve and its therapies is important. This feedback helps you to assess the effectiveness of your communication and refine your educational approaches. Encouraging patients to share their thoughts and questions can provide insights into common areas of confusion or interest, allowing you to tailor future discussions and materials to meet their needs better. This continual feedback loop and adjustment help build a more informed, engaged patient community empowered to take active roles in their health management.

By creating a deeper understanding of the vagus nerve among patients, you enhance their capacity to manage their health more effectively and enrich your therapeutic relationship. Through thoughtful communication, supportive educational materials, personalized consultations, and responsive feedback mechanisms, you can illuminate the vagus nerve's role in overall health, inspiring patients to embrace informed, proactive steps toward wellness. This approach transforms individual health outcomes and advances the broader mission of healthcare—to empower each individual with the knowledge and tools necessary for optimal health.

SOMATIC EXERCISES FOR PATIENT RECOMMENDATIONS

In the therapeutic landscape, somatic exercises emerge as a gentle yet powerful tool to enhance physical and mental well-being. These exercises, which focus on the mind-body connection, are efficient in stimulating the vagus nerve, promoting relaxation, and reducing symptoms of various disorders. As a practitioner, selecting and teaching these exercises with consideration for individual patient needs enhances the treatment's effectiveness and ensures patient safety and engagement.

When recommending somatic exercises, try to tailor your approach based on each patient's medical history and current health status. Begin by conducting a thorough assessment, considering factors such as the patient's mobility, pain levels, and specific symptoms or conditions like anxiety or digestive issues. For instance, a patient with lower back pain might benefit from gentle pelvic tilts and knee-to-chest stretches, which can help alleviate discomfort without straining the back. On the other hand, someone experiencing high stress levels might find diaphragmatic breathing and guided relaxation more beneficial in activating their vagus nerve and creating a calm state.

Instruction techniques are important in the effectiveness of somatic exercises. Clear, step-by-step demonstrations are essential. Begin by explaining the purpose of each exercise—how it impacts the body, particularly the vagus nerve, and the expected benefits. Demonstrate each movement slowly, emphasizing proper form and breathing patterns. Encourage patients to mirror these actions while you watch closely to correct any misalignments or adjustments needed to perform the exercises safely and effectively. It's also helpful to provide visual aids or handouts that patients can refer to when practicing independently, reinforcing the correct techniques and sequences.

Integrating somatic exercises into a patient's overall treatment plan requires thoughtful consideration of their daily routines and physical capabilities. Discuss with patients how they can incorporate these practices into their everyday lives. For instance, I recommend engaging in short neck stretches or mindful breathing exercises during work breaks to reduce tension and boost focus. Establish a realistic frequency and duration for these exercises, starting with shorter sessions to build the patient's confidence and comfort level. Gradually increase the duration as their proficiency improves. Regular follow-ups are essential to assess progress and adjust the exercise regimen, ensuring it remains aligned with their evolving health needs.

Adapting exercises for special populations is necessary for inclusive care. For elderly patients or those with mobility limitations, modifications might be necessary to accommodate their physical capabilities. Chair yoga, for example, can be an excellent alternative, providing the benefits of muscle stretching and relaxation without the need to get down on the floor. Similarly, for patients with neurological conditions that affect balance, exercises that can be performed lying down or with the support of a wall are safer and more feasible. Always consider using props like chairs, cushions, or straps to assist with performing the exercises safely and effectively.

In this discussion of somatic exercises for patient recommendations, we have looked at the careful selection of exercises tailored to individual needs, effective instructional techniques, thoughtful integration into treatment plans, and necessary adaptations for special populations. By approaching somatic exercises with a nuanced understanding of each patient's unique health landscape, you, as a healthcare provider, can significantly enhance the therapeutic experience, promoting physical relief and a more profound sense of wellness and empowerment among your patients. Through these mindful practices, the potential for healing and rejuvenation is enormous, underscoring the critical role of the mind-body connection in achieving overall health and vitality.

MEASURING VAGAL TONE IN CLINICAL PRACTICE

In the intricate dance of body systems where harmony equates to health, the vagus nerve plays a major role as a conductor of this physiological orchestra. Understanding and measuring this nerve's efficacy, or vagal tone, is more than a technical assessment—it is a gauge of overall well-being. Vagal tone isn't just a marker; it's also a predictor, offering insights into a patient's resilience in the face of stress, capacity for emotional regulation, and potential recovery paths from physical ailments. It's essential, therefore, that as a clinician, you know how to measure this vital function and interpret and act upon the data with precision and empathy.

The primary method for assessing vagal tone is through heart rate variability (HRV). This measurement isn't about the speed of the heart rate but rather the variation in intervals between heartbeats. A higher HRV indicates a robust vagal tone, signifying a better ability to adapt to stress and maintain internal balance. Conversely, a lower HRV can signal weakened vagal activity and often coincides with higher susceptibility to stress and disease. Techniques to measure HRV range from sophisticated medical devices used in clinical settings to wearable technology that patients can use in everyday life. These provide useful data that can guide treatment options and lifestyle recommendations.

Another valuable measure is respiratory sinus arrhythmia (RSA). This technique involves observing how heart rate changes with breathing. During inhalation, the heart rate typically speeds up and it slows down upon exhalation. The higher the vagal tone, the more significant the difference between the heart rate during inhalation and exhalation. RSA provides a snapshot of autonomic nervous system balance and offers a window into how well the body can manage and recover from stress.

Interpreting these measurements requires a nuanced under-standing of the numbers and the individual patient's overall health context. For instance, a sudden drop in HRV could indicate a recent stressor or a change in health status, prompting a need for adjustment in therapy or further investigation. Conversely, an improvement in HRV or RSA scores over time can positively affirm the current treatment approach, be it through medication, therapy, or lifestyle changes. This data-driven approach allows you to tailor interventions more precisely and monitor their effective-ness with concrete evidence, enhancing the quality of care.

Let's incorporate a case study into this narrative. Consider the story of a middle-aged patient with chronic anxiety who exhibited a notably low HRV at the outset of treatment. Through a combination of vagus nerve stimulation (VNS) therapy, tailored medication, and guided breathing exercises, significant improvements in HRV were observed over several months. Each clinical visit provided an opportunity to review real-time data, adjust treatments, and discuss progress, empowering the patient with knowledge and involvement in their healing process. This case highlighted the important role of regular vagal tone assessments. It demonstrated the potential for personalized, adaptive treatment plans based on real-time physiological data.

As you continue to engage with patients, remember that measuring vagal tone informs a broader strategy to enhance the intricate connection between mind and body. By mastering these measurement techniques and integrating them into your clinical practice, you equip yourself with the ability to see beneath the surface of symptoms to the underlying autonomic narratives, enabling a deeper, more effective approach to health and healing. With each assessment and patient interaction, you are tuning into the very rhythms that dictate human wellness.

CASE STUDIES: SUCCESS STORIES FROM THE FIELD

In the evolving landscape of medical treatments where personal stories and clinical data intertwine, the narrative of vagus nerve therapy unfolds through the lives it has touched and transformed. Each case reinforces the potential of vagus nerve interventions and enriches our understanding of its application across diverse conditions. By examining specific instances where vagus nerve therapies have significantly altered patient outcomes, we gain insights into the practical aspects of these treatments and their profound impact on individuals' lives.

Consider the story of Maria, a 42-year-old woman diagnosed with refractory epilepsy. Despite numerous medications, her seizures remained frequent and unpredictable, casting a shadow over her independence and quality of life. Her neurologist suggested a trial of vagus nerve stimulation as a last resort. The decision wasn't made lightly, but the potential to regain some normalcy was compelling. Six months post-implantation of a VNS device, her seizure frequency dropped by over 70%. This improvement allowed Maria to return to her job and restored a sense of control over her life. Maria's case is a testament to the targeted effectiveness of VNS in epilepsy management, especially for those who have exhausted other treatment avenues. This example highlights the necessity of staying abreast of patient responses and being prepared to suggest alternative treatments when traditional methods falter.

Transitioning from neurological disorders to mental health, consider James, a veteran suffering from severe, treatment-resistant depression. Conventional antidepressants and therapy sessions had offered little relief, and his condition remained stagnant. James was allowed to try transcutaneous vagus nerve stimulation (tVNS), a non-invasive method applied through the ear, as part of a pilot study. Over several weeks of consistent treatment, there was a notable improvement in his mood and functionality. James reported feeling more present in his interactions and started engaging in activities he had avoided for years. His case illuminates the potential of VNS to revolutionize treatment paradigms for depression, particularly highlighting the importance of integrating new scientific findings into clinical practice rapidly.

Another compelling story comes from Lisa, who was battling rheumatoid arthritis, characterized by debilitating pain and joint damage. Alongside her standard immunosuppressive therapy, her rheumatologist suggested adjunctive vagus nerve stimulation to help manage her pain. The rationale was based on emerging research linking the anti-inflammatory effects of VNS with improvements in autoimmune conditions. After regular sessions, Lisa experienced significant pain relief and a reduction in her reliance on painkillers, which had numerous unpleasant side effects. Her improved physical capabilities enabled her to engage more actively in physical therapy, enhancing her mobility and quality of life. This case underscores the multifaceted benefits of VNS, as a direct treatment and as a complementary approach that can amplify the effects of other therapies.

Lastly, consider the collective experience of a group of patients in a geriatric care facility suffering from chronic digestive issues, a common problem exacerbated by their limited mobility and existing health conditions. Incorporating a daily regimen of light somatic exercises designed to stimulate the vagus nerve led to noticeable improvements in their digestion and general health. This simple yet effective intervention highlighted how non-invasive vagus nerve therapies can enhance gastrointestinal function, a crucial aspect of health, especially in the elderly population. This collective case study provided a blueprint for similar interventions in other facilities. It demonstrated vagus nerve-focused therapies' broad applicability and scalability across different care settings.

Each of these stories demonstrates the potential and versatility of vagus nerve therapies. From reducing seizures and alleviating depression to managing chronic pain and improving digestive health, the implications are vast. These case studies serve as foundational building blocks for future treatment strategies, offering inspiration and practical insights into integrating vagus nerve therapies into diverse clinical practices. As these stories continue to accumulate, they give us a deeper understanding and broader acceptance of vagus nerve stimulation as a critical component of modern medical practice, promising new horizons for patient care and therapeutic innovation.

ETHICAL CONSIDERATIONS IN VAGUS NERVE THERAPY

In medical treatment, particularly with innovations like vagus nerve stimulation (VNS), the ethical landscape is as vast and complex as the clinical one. Practitioners are tasked with healing yet must at all times maintain their ethical integrity, especially when using emerging therapies. The cornerstone of good ethics is informed consent, necessary for legal compliance and for fostering trust and respect between you and your patients.

Informed consent goes beyond simply getting a patient to sign a form; it involves having an open dialogue wherein the patient is fully apprised of the potential risks and benefits of VNS. This conversation is even more important when dealing with newer or less conventional treatments where patient familiarity might be lacking. You must ensure they understand the treatment, potential outcomes, and possible side effects. Transparency here is key. For instance, while discussing VNS, explain its proven benefits, like reduced seizure frequency in epilepsy, and its risks, such as possible throat discomfort or voice alterations due to nerve stimulation. This honest communication empowers patients to make informed decisions. It solidifies their trust in the medical process, knowing their health and autonomy are valued.

When explaining the potential risks and benefits, try to maintain a balance between hope and realism. VNS can offer significant improvements in quality of life for individuals with treatment-resistant depression or chronic pain, but it is not a guaranteed cure. Discussing the variability in patient responses helps set realistic expectations, which is important for patient satisfaction and can impact their overall treatment experience. On the flip side, highlighting the potential life-enhancing benefits of VNS can provide hope and motivation for patients, especially those who have struggled with persistent symptoms despite trying various treatments. This balanced approach aids in informed decision-making and aligns with your ethical duty to provide care that enhances life quality.

Adhering to the regulatory standards and guidelines for using VNS is another element of ethical practice. These regulations safeguard patient safety and ensure treatments are based on sound scientific evidence. Staying updated with these standards helps maintain compliance and assures patients that their treatments meet nationally and internationally accepted safety criteria. Attending regular training sessions and seminars, and staying engaged with professional bodies can keep you at the forefront of regulatory updates and clinical best practices.

Lastly, cultural sensitivity must be addressed. Our global society is a mixture of beliefs and values, and medical treatment, including VNS, is perceived through the lens of these cultural backgrounds. Some patients may have reservations about "artificial" or "invasive" treatments due to cultural beliefs or previous experiences with healthcare. Addressing these concerns with sensitivity and respect involves:

- Listening earnestly to their concerns
- Providing information that respects their cultural perspectives
- Adapting treatment plans to better align with their cultural or personal values

In summary, the ethical considerations in vagus nerve therapy are multifaceted and integral to modern medicine. They require engagement with patients, staying informed about legal and regulatory standards, and approaching each treatment with the sensitivity that respects the diverse cultures represented within the patient population.

CHAPTER 8: BUILDING A COMMUNITY OF VAGAL TONE ADVOCATES

I magine the power of a single voice becoming a chorus, each note harmonizing to create a symphony of awareness and support. This is the essence of building a community around the vital yet often overlooked topic of vagal tone. We've explored the potential of the vagus nerve in promoting health and well-being. The next step is to foster a community where knowledge, support, and experiences are shared freely—a community of vagal tone advocates.

STARTING A LOCAL SUPPORT GROUP

Steps to Initiate

The journey of starting a local support group begins with clarity and intention. The first step is to scout the right location—a space that is accessible and welcoming, such as a community center, library, or even a quiet park. This physical space needs to resonate with safety and comfort, as it will be the place where members feel encouraged to share and grow. After securing a location, the next step is to organize initial meetups. These can be informal gatherings, perhaps starting with a small group of interested individuals. The key here is consistency; decide on regular intervals—weekly or monthly—to meet, ensuring the group gains momentum and maintains engagement.

Group Structure and Meetings

Structuring the group involves thoughtful consideration of how each session will be conducted. Begin by setting clear agendas for each meeting, which might include discussions on the latest research, personal sharing segments, and guest speaker sessions. Create an environment where all members can speak freely and without judgment. This nurturing atmosphere can be cultivated by establishing ground rules that promote respectful listening and confidentiality. Each meeting should ideally end with a collective reflection or group activity that reinforces the session's theme, enhancing the sense of community and shared purpose.

Engagement Activities

Engagement is the lifeblood of any support group. Activities should be diverse and inclusive, catering to the interests and capacities of all group members. Consider inviting guest speakers such as healthcare professionals or experienced practitioners who can provide deeper insights into the vagus nerve and its impact on health. Organizing workshops or small group discussions can also be incredibly beneficial as they allow members to explore topics more interactively. Activities such as guided group meditations or breathing exercises educate and provide practical tools that members can take away and incorporate into their daily routines.

Resources and Management Tools

Effectively managing a support group requires organization and access to the right tools. Utilizing digital platforms for communication, such as emails or a dedicated Facebook group, can help disseminate information and keep the community engaged between meetings. For scheduling, tools like Google Calendar or Doodle can simplify the coordination of meeting times that suit all members. Additionally, maintaining a repository of resources— articles, videos, and book recommendations—on a shared drive or online platform can be invaluable. These tools support the logistical aspects of managing the group and enrich the members' experience by providing continuous learning and engagement opportunities.

Creating and nurturing a community around vagal tone advocacy is a profound way to amplify the impact of individual efforts and foster a supportive network that can significantly enhance its members' well-being. Through shared experiences, continuous learning, and collective support, such a community becomes a powerhouse of transformative change, echoing the benefits of understanding and improving one's vagus nerve function far beyond its initial members.

ONLINE RESOURCES AND SOCIAL MEDIA FOR VAGUS NERVE HEALTH

In the expansive digital age, where information and community are at our fingertips, online platforms can significantly enhance our efforts to spread awareness and knowledge about the vagus nerve. With its vast reach, social media provides an excellent avenue to share valuable insights, connect with like-minded individuals, and build a community focused on promoting vagal health. Platforms such as Facebook, Instagram, and Twitter offer opportunities to engage with audiences through various forms of content, from informative posts and live discussions to interactive polls and stories. By consistently sharing well-researched content, personal experiences, and expert insights, you can create a vibrant online community that supports education and discussion about the vagus nerve's crucial role in health and wellness.

Creating a dedicated blog or website about vagus nerve health can be a central hub for all your educational materials, articles, videos, and resources. This establishes your credibility in the field and provides a structured space for people to learn and explore at their own pace. When setting up a blog, focus on user-friendly design and navigation to ensure visitors can easily find the information they need. Incorporate basic Search Engine Optimization (SEO) strategies such as using relevant keywords, creating quality content regularly, and ensuring your site is mobile-friendly to improve visibility and attract more visitors. Engaging content that answers common questions or explores intriguing facets of the vagus nerve can encourage visitors to return, fostering a loyal following.

The internet is also home to numerous forums and online communities where individuals gather to share experiences and support one another. Platforms like Reddit, Quora, and specific health forums provide spaces where questions can be asked and knowledge shared freely. Participating in these communities by providing thoughtful answers and sharing experiences can raise awareness about the importance of the vagus nerve. Creating a dedicated online group or forum can facilitate more focused discussions and provide a support network for individuals seeking to improve their vagal tone through lifestyle changes, exercises, and other therapies.

When it comes to engaging an online audience, digital content strategies are important. Visual content, such as infographics and short videos, tends to capture attention effectively and can be used to explain complex topics like vagus nerve functions or breathing exercises engagingly. Interactive posts, such as quizzes about vagus nerve health or interactive webinars, can also increase engagement and learning. By regularly updating your social media platforms and blog with fresh, relevant content, you can keep the audience interested and motivated to learn more. Additionally, encourage user interaction by asking questions, soliciting feedback, and creating content that responds to the audience's interests and needs.

Embracing the power of digital tools and platforms to promote understanding and knowledge about the vagus nerve broadens the reach of your advocacy. It enriches the quality of information and support available to individuals worldwide. This approach leverages technology to nurture a global community united by a common interest in health and wellness, amplifying the impact of your efforts and contributing to a greater understanding of how we can all harness the potential of our vagus nerve for a healthier life.

HOSTING WORKSHOPS AND SEMINARS

Hosting a workshop or seminar can feel overwhelming but meticulous planning and organization sets the stage for a successful and impactful gathering. To start, select relevant and compelling topics that resonate with your audience's interests and needs related to the vagus nerve and its influence on health. This choice determines the framework of your entire event. Once the topics have been chosen, identify and invite speakers who are both knowledgeable and engaging. These experts could be healthcare professionals, experienced practitioners, or well-informed advocates of vagal tone health.

The logistics of organizing such an event include securing a venue that is accessible and conducive to learning. This space should have the necessary audio-visual equipment and comfortable seating arrangements to facilitate an optimal learning environment. Following this, strategize the event's marketing to ensure a good turnout. Utilize various platforms such as social media, community bulletins, and email newsletters to advertise the seminar. Include precise details about the topics, speakers, date, time, and how to register. Early bird registration or discounts for groups can incentivize early sign-ups and help gauge the number of attendees in advance.

Incorporate various engaging elements to create a dynamic and interactive atmosphere during the workshop. Live demonstrations of techniques such as breathing exercises or guided meditations stimulating the vagus nerve can be particularly effective. These keep the audience engaged and provide practical skills attendees can take home. Additionally, setting aside time for question-and-answer sessions can encourage interaction and allow a deeper exploration of the subjects discussed. Hands-on activities, where participants can practice or simulate techniques under the guidance of experts, also enrich the learning experience, making the theoretical knowledge gained more tangible and applicable.

Follow-up after the event is important. Gathering feedback through surveys or informal conversations can provide insights into what participants found most valuable and what could be improved for future seminars. This feedback will help you refine the content and delivery of subsequent events. Maintaining contact with attendees through follow-up emails that include additional resources, session recordings, or upcoming event announcements can keep the community engaged and invested in their journey toward understanding and improving their vagus nerve health.

Collaborating with guest speakers is another facet of hosting workshops that can significantly enhance the value of the event. When selecting speakers, look for individuals who not only bring expertise but also a passion for education and a willingness to interact with attendees. Before the event, collaborate with them to ensure their presentations align with your overall objectives for the seminar and are tailored to the audience's level of understanding. Giving speakers feedback from previous events can also help them fine-tune their presentations to meet the audience's expectations better.

By meticulously planning and organizing, integrating interactive elements, and effectively collaborating with knowledgeable speakers, your workshops or seminars can become wonderful experiences for participants. Through these educational gatherings, you can extend the reach of vital health information, facilitating a collective rise in awareness and advocacy that could ripple into wider community health improvements.

CREATING ENGAGING CONTENT FOR COMMUNITY EDUCATION

In this digital age, where information is just a click away, the challenge doesn't lie in finding content but in ensuring it connects and resonates with the audience. When educating our community about something as intricate and vital as vagal tone, the approach to creating educational materials must be thoughtful and engaging. Use a variety of tools such as pamphlets, newsletters, and e-books each tailored to explain facets of the vagus nerve.

Let's talk about pamphlets first. These can serve as quick, easy-to-digest guides on specific aspects of the vagus nerve, such as its role in managing stress or improving digestion. They should be concise, well-structured, and visually appealing, making them perfect for grabbing attention at workshops or health fairs. Pictures help a lot as people tend to avoid long paragraphs of text only.

Next, newsletters offer a more regular touchpoint with your community. They can provide updates on the latest research, share personal stories of those benefiting from vagal tone exercises, and offer tips for incorporating these practices into daily routines.

E-books allow for a deeper dive. They can cover comprehensive guides on exercises to stimulate the vagus nerve, detailed explanations of its functions, and interviews with experts in the field. These digital books are wonderful resources for those who wish to explore the subject matter more thoroughly at their own pace.

Visual aids are indispensable when discussing subjects as abstract and complex as neurological functions. Charts detailing the path of the vagus nerve, models showing its interaction with various organs, and diagrams explaining neurobiological processes can transform complicated abstract concepts into simple, easily grasped concepts. Visual learning aids enhance comprehension and retention, making them perfect for workshops where a lot of information is covered in a short time. They help attendees visualize and remember the key points long after the workshop ends.

Handouts are another useful resource, particularly during seminars and workshops. These should include key points from presentations, space for personal notes, and quick exercises or quizzes to encourage interaction with the material. Handouts can guide discussions, provide reference points, and serve as reminders of the learning objectives.

Finally, making content accessible is crucial in ensuring it benefits everyone. This means considering your audience's language, literacy levels, and digital access. Clear, simple language free from medical jargon can make the materials more understandable for most people. Providing printed copies or options to receive information via mail will benefit those with limited internet access. In digital formats, ensuring that your content is compatible with screen readers and providing subtitles for videos can make your resources more accessible to those with visual or hearing impairments.

COLLABORATING WITH WELLNESS PROFESSIONALS

In the health and wellness world, often each practitioner holds a piece of the larger puzzle of human health. Establishing robust networks with such wellness professionals is essential. You need to create a network of health resources where therapists, dietitians, yoga instructors, and other specialists can contribute their expertise, creating a more comprehensive approach to enhancing vagal tone and overall well-being. Building these professional networks involves reaching out, nurturing relationships, and sharing knowledge that can elevate our practices and the lives of those we serve.

The process begins with identifying and connecting with professionals whose expertise and practices align with the principles of vagal nerve health. To find them, you may need to attend networking events, participate in health and wellness conferences, or join professional associations that offer access to a broader network of health practitioners. When reaching out, consider the mutual benefits of the connection. For instance, a dietitian specializing in gut health could greatly benefit from understanding the role of the vagus nerve in digestive processes, just as your understanding of nutritional impacts on vagal tone could be deepened through this collaboration. These relationships are built on mutual respect and a shared goal of improving patient care, making them enduring and mutually beneficial.

Engaging in joint ventures is a powerful strategy to broaden the reach and impact of your advocacy for vagal nerve health. Consider co-hosting events, where each professional can bring their unique perspective and expertise to the table. For example, organizing a workshop on holistic health that combines your insights into vagal tone with a yoga instructor's expertise in physical poses that stimulate the vagus nerve and a therapist's techniques for managing stress and anxiety. These collaborative projects will provide a richer, more holistic experience for participants and showcase the interdisciplinary approach needed for effective health management. Cross-promotion of services, such as featuring one another's work on social media platforms or during community talks, can further extend your reach, attracting a wider audience who can benefit from a more integrated approach to health.

Gaining professional endorsements is another way to enhance your work's credibility and visibility. When respected professionals in the health community publicly support your advocacy, it lends credibility that can attract more community members and open doors to broader opportunities, such as funding for research or invitations to speak at major conferences. Securing these endorsements involves showcasing the effectiveness and scientific backing of your approaches. Providing evidence-based information and demonstrating successful outcomes from your practices can encourage other professionals to endorse and support your work.

Continuing education remains a cornerstone of effective collaboration and advocacy. Staying updated on the latest research and advancements in the field of vagus nerve health allows you to bring fresh, relevant, and scientifically-backed information to your community and professional network. This can be achieved through subscribing to relevant medical journals, attending specialized training sessions, and participating in ongoing professional development courses. By continuously educating yourself, you maintain your role as a knowledgeable leader in the field, inspiring confidence and trust in your peers and the communities you serve. Moreover, sharing this updated knowledge with your network through organized meet-ups or professional newsletters reinforces your commitment to the field and encourages a culture of learning and growth among your peers.

Through thoughtful networking, collaborative projects, professional endorsements, and a commitment to ongoing education, you can significantly amplify the impact of your work on vagal nerve health. By uniting with other professionals, you'll harness a wealth of knowledge and experience, paving the way for innovative health solutions and transformative community health outcomes.

FUTURE DIRECTIONS IN VAGUS NERVE RESEARCH AND ADVOCACY

As we stand on the brink of discoveries in the study of the vagus nerve, it's thrilling to consider how emerging research could redefine what we know about our body's capabilities for self-regulation and healing. Recent investigations into vagal tone are uncovering its potential to impact a wide array of health conditions, from inflammatory diseases to psychiatric disorders. These studies are expanding our knowledge and opening doors to innovative treatments that could transform lives. For instance, ongoing research into bioelectronic medicine—a field that includes vagus nerve stimulation (VNS)—is showing promise in treating rheumatoid arthritis and depression, conditions that can be resistant to traditional therapies. This cutting-edge research underscores the necessity of continued exploration and support in this area, as each finding brings the potential for significant breakthroughs in medical science and holistic health practices.

In advocating for more research and funding, our approach must be as multifaceted as the nerve we study. It begins with raising awareness about the importance of this research, not just among scientists and medical professionals but also within the broader community and among policymakers who can drive funding decisions. Highlighting the tangible benefits of increased research into the vagus nerve can catalyze interest and action. One way is to share success stories of individuals whose quality of life has dramatically improved due to VNS. Additionally, aligning with professional organizations that can lend their influential voices to this cause can amplify our efforts, turning the whisper of our advocacy into a roar that cannot be ignored.

Expanding the impact our community's impact involves forging partnerships with key stakeholders in the health and wellness sector. Collaborating with educational institutions can facilitate the integration of vagus nerve studies into health curricula, creating a new generation of healthcare professionals who are knowledgeable about its potential. Engaging with healthcare providers to share emerging research and practical applications can enhance the quality of care and broaden the acceptance and use of vagus nerve therapies. Moreover, working alongside policymakers to advocate for supportive legislation and funding can ensure that vagus nerve research receives the attention and resources it deserves.

Sustaining momentum in this field requires continuous engagement and celebration of achievements. Recognizing milestones in research and therapy developments can motivate and inform the community. Regular updates through newsletters or social media can keep the excitement alive and stakeholders engaged. Setting long-term goals with clear benchmarks for success can provide ongoing direction and purpose for the community's efforts. Celebrating these successes fuels our collective drive and reminds us of our progress toward a deeper understanding and broader application of vagus nerve therapies.

As we look to the future, the potential for research and advocacy in vagus nerve health holds immense promise. With each study, each collaboration, and each success, we are advancing scientific knowledge and enhancing the well-being of countless individuals. Our work now lays the foundation for a healthier, more resilient society, and our shared commitment and passion will drive this mission forward. Let's continue to advocate, educate, and innovate as we unlock the full potential of the vagus nerve in promoting holistic health.

SPREAD THE WORD!

Not many people understand how important the vagus nerve is or the role it plays in the body. We can change that simply by talking about it and sharing information—and here's your chance to do just that!

Simply by sharing your honest opinion of this book and a little about your own experience, you'll show new readers where they can find this information and the techniques that could help them feel so much better.

Thank you so much for your support. I truly appreciate it.

Scan the QR code to leave your review on Amazon.

Scan me!

CONCLUSION

As we draw this book to a close, I want to thank you for accompanying me on this enlightening journey—together we've explored the immense capabilities of the vagus nerve and your own potential for healing and growth. We've looked closely at how the vagus nerve influences our mental, physical, and emotional well-being.

Throughout these pages, we've explored various facets of the vagus nerve—its essential functions, the impact of its stimulation on our health, and the power of simple, everyday practices that can significantly enhance our lives. From practical somatic exercises tailored for daily routines to specialized techniques to easing anxiety and stress, each chapter has built upon the foundation of understanding and activating this remarkable aspect of our biology. We've discussed how nurturing gut health and addressing chronic pain through vagal stimulation can lead to profound improvements and how incorporating mind-body therapies can holistically enrich our lives.

The key takeaway from our time together is clear: small, consistent actions can lead to substantial changes. The mind-body connection is powerful, and by engaging in practices that stimulate the vagus nerve, you are taking control of your health in a deeply impactful way. Remember, these benefits are accessible to everyone, regardless of your health background or current physical condition.

Now, I encourage you to integrate these insights into your daily life. Start with one or two techniques that resonate with you, and as you grow more comfortable and see the positive changes, gradually incorporate more practices. Each small step is a leap towards enhanced well-being.

I also urge you to share your journey and the knowledge you've gained. Talk about the vagus nerve with friends and family, or consider starting a community group where you can practice together.

I commend you for your openness to new ideas and your commitment to improving your health. This path is a continuous journey of self-discovery and improvement.

My sincere thanks for investing your time and energy into exploring the potential of your vagus nerve with me. I am grateful for your presence on this path and excited about the possibilities ahead for you.

For further information, to ask questions, or to join a community of like-minded individuals, please visit my website or follow me on social media. Also, keep an eye out for upcoming workshops, webinars, and speaking engagements, where we can dive even deeper into the practices and principles discussed in this book. Together, let's continue to explore, share, and grow. Here's to your health and the exciting journey that awaits us all!

With deepest gratitude, Nicole Reap

VAGUS NERVE HEALTH QUIZ

This quiz has been designed to help you understand the importance and functions of the vagus nerve and how to keep it healthy!

1. What is the primary function of the vagus nerve?

  a) Heart rate control
  b) Digestion regulation
  c) Breathing control
  d) All of the above

2. Where does the vagus nerve originate?

  a) Cerebellum
  b) Brainstem
  c) Spinal cord
  d) Cerebrum

3. Which of the following activities is known to stimulate the vagus nerve?

a) Singing or humming
b) Intense physical exercise
c) Holding your breath
d) Drinking coffee

4. The vagus nerve plays a crucial role in which part of the autonomic nervous system?

a) Sympathetic nervous system
b) Parasympathetic nervous system
c) Central nervous system
d) Peripheral nervous system

5. True or False: The vagus nerve only affects the digestive system.

a) True
b) False

6. Which breathing technique is often used to stimulate the vagus nerve?

a) Rapid, shallow breathing
b) Deep, slow breathing
c) Holding your breath for as long as possible
d) Panting

7. What impact does stimulating the vagus nerve have on heart rate?

a) Increases heart rate

b) Decreases heart rate

c) Has no effect on heart rate

d) Causes irregular heartbeats

8. Which of the following is NOT a potential benefit of vagus nerve stimulation?

a) Improved digestion

b) Reduced inflammation

c) Increased anxiety

d) Enhanced mood

9. What common yoga pose is known to stimulate the vagus nerve?

a) Child's Pose

b) Tree Pose

c) Downward Dog

d) Warrior II

10. Which of the following foods can help support vagus nerve health?

a) Processed foods

b) Sugary drinks

c) Fermented foods

d) Fried foods

Answers:

1. d) All of the above
2. b) Brainstem
3. a) Singing or humming
4. b) Parasympathetic nervous system
5. b) False
6. b) Deep, slow breathing
7. b) Decreases heart rate
8. c) Increased anxiety
9. a) Child's Pose
10. c) Fermented foods

REFERENCES

"The 100 Best Wellness and Wellbeing Quotes." La Macchina. Accessed September 24, 2024. https://www.la-macchina.ch/portfolio/the-best-wellness-healt-quotes

The polyvagal theory: New insights into adaptive reactions ... https://www.ncbi.nlm.nih.gov/pmc/articles/PMC3108032/

Vagus Nerve: Function, Stimulation, and More https://www.healthline.com/human-body-maps/vagus-nerve

Methods of assessing vagus nerve activity and reflexes https://www.ncbi.nlm.nih.gov/pmc/articles/PMC4322860/

Vagus Nerve Exercises: 4 Ways to Handle Stress https://apolloneuro.com/blogs/news/4-vagus-nerve-exercises-to-transform-how-you-handle-stress

5 Ways To Stimulate Your Vagus Nerve https://health.clevelandclinic.org/vagus-nerve-stimulation

Somatic Exercises for Anxiety: Relieve Stress and Tension ... https://compassionify.com/somatic-exercises-for-anxiety/

Diaphragmatic Breathing and Its Benefits https://www.healthline.com/health/diaphragmatic-breathing

Dynamic Stretching Strategies for Desk Professionals https://www.stretchxco.com/elevate-your-workday-dynamic-stretching-strategies-for-desk-professionals

Bolster Your Brain by Stimulating the Vagus Nerve https://www.cedars-sinai.org/blog/stimulating-the-vagus-nerve.html

Humming (Simple Bhramari Pranayama) as a Stress Buster https://www.ncbi.nlm.nih.gov/pmc/articles/PMC10182780/

Effects of Cold Stimulation on Cardiac-Vagal Activation in ... https://www.ncbi.nlm.nih.gov/pmc/articles/PMC6334714/

How to Build a Better Bedtime Routine for Adults https://www.sleepfoundation.org/sleep-hygiene/bedtime-routine-for-adults

Vagus Nerve Stimulation at the Interface of Brain–Gut ... https://www.ncbi.nlm.nih.gov/pmc/articles/PMC6671930/

The Potential Effects of Probiotics and ω-3 Fatty Acids on ... https://www.ncbi.nlm.nih.gov/pmc/articles/PMC7468753/

How Somatic Exercise Can Heal Your Gut Issues https://theworkoutwitch.-com/blogs/news/how-somatic-exercise-can-heal-your-gut-issues-for-good

Mindful Eating: A Review Of How The Stress-Digestion ... https://www.ncbi.nlm.nih.gov/pmc/articles/PMC7219460/

Vagus nerve stimulation https://www.mayoclinic.org/tests-procedures/vagus-nerve-stimulation/about/pac-20384565

The effect of an anti-inflammatory diet on chronic pain https://www.ncbi.nlm.nih.gov/pmc/articles/PMC10381948/

The vagus nerve and the inflammatory reflex—linking ... https://www.ncbi.nlm.nih.gov/pmc/articles/PMC4082307/

Somatic Therapy: Benefits, Types And Efficacy https://www.forbes.-com/health/mind/somatic-therapy/

Efficacy of Biofeedback for Medical Conditions https://www.ncbi.nlm.nih.-gov/pmc/articles/PMC6854143/

Reset Your Nervous System: Somatic Tools for Vagal Tone https://www.somatopi-a.com/blog/reset-your-nervous-system-somatic-tools-for-vagal-tone

Eight Visualization Techniques For Stress Reduction https://www.betterhelp.-com/advice/stress/9-visualization-techniques-for-stress-reduction/

Breath of Life: The Respiratory Vagal Stimulation Model ... https://www.ncbi.nlm.nih.gov/pmc/articles/PMC6189422/

Vagus nerve stimulation https://www.mayoclinic.org/tests-procedures/vagus-nerve-stimulation/about/pac-20384565

Reset Your Nervous System: Somatic Tools for Vagal Tone https://www.somatopi-a.com/blog/reset-your-nervous-system-somatic-tools-for-vagal-tone

Methods of assessing vagus nerve activity and reflexes https://www.ncbi.nlm.nih.gov/pmc/articles/PMC4322860/

Neuroethics of Neuromodulation: An Update - PMC https://www.ncbi.nlm.nih.-gov/pmc/articles/PMC6345549/

Guide to Starting a Support Group https://iocdf.org/ocd-finding-help/support-groups/how-to-start-a-support-group/

Use of Social Media for Health Advocacy for Digital ... https://www.ncbi.nlm.nih.-gov/pmc/articles/PMC10685274/

5 Essential Steps in Developing Successful Wellness ...https://incentfit.com/well ness-word/5-essential-steps-to-develop-successful-wellness-programs/ -

Exploring the potential of vagus nerve stimulation in ...https://eurjmedres.biomed central.com/articles/10.1186/s40001-023-01439-2

ABOUT THE AUTHOR

Nicole Reap is a passionate advocate for holistic healing and personal empowerment. With an extensive background in somatic therapy and vagus nerve stimulation, Nicole blends her knowledge of the body's innate healing abilities with a deep understanding of spiritual and emotional well-being. Her studies in chakras, energy flow, and spiritual practices complement her work in healing, offering a comprehensive approach that addresses both physical and emotional health.

Nicole's journey into holistic and spiritual studies began alongside her teaching and entrepreneur careers. With years of experience in finance and business, she has now expanded her focus to include the powerful connection between mind, body, and spirit. Her books, including "Somatic Therapy for Beginners" and "Vagus Nerve Vitality," provide practical tools for readers to explore healing on all levels.

Dedicated to making complex topics accessible, Nicole weaves together science, spirituality, and self-help in a way that resonates with both beginners and seasoned practitioners. She believes understanding our bodies, emotions, and energy is vital to living a balanced and empowered life.